FREEDOM FIGHTERS

By the same Author

Eminent Indians:
FREEDOM FIGHTERS

M.L. Ahuja

Rupa & Co

Copyright © M.L. Ahuja 2006

Published 2006 by

Rupa & Co

7/16, Ansari Road, Daryaganj,
New Delhi 110 002

Sales Centres:

Allahabad Bangalore Chandigarh Chennai
Hyderabad Jaipur Kathmandu
Kolkata Mumbai Pune

Typeset in 11 pts Revival by
Nikita Overseas Pvt. Ltd.
1410 Chiranjiv Tower
43 Nehru Place
New Delhi 110 019

Printed in India by
Saurabh Printers Pvt. Ltd.
A-16 Sector-IV
Noida 201 301

My parents who, though no more,
have been the source of inspiration to me

Contents

Preface

*I*ndia attained independence almost 58 years back on 15 August 1947. Old generation has virtually withered away and the new one has blossomed. It is, therefore, an appropriate time to introduce precisely the history of the struggle waged by the people of India to achieve this freedom. The succeeding generations should know the trials and tribulations our ancestors had to face and sacrifices made by many of them.

Jawaharlal Nehru in his first address to the nation, as first Prime Minister of Independent India, said:

> Long years ago, we made a tryst with destiny and now the time comes when we shall redeem our pledge, not wholly or in full measure, but very substantially. At the stroke of the midnight hour, when the world sleeps, India will awake to life and freedom.

What was this 'tryst with destiny' about which Nehru was speaking. He was obviously referring to his resolve for *'Purna Swaraj'*, full and total Independence, made on 31 December

1929, as President of the Indian National Congress while unfurling the tri-colour on the banks of the river Ravi in Lahore.

But the struggle to which Nehru's speech referred to did not start in 1929. This struggle for emancipation from the colonial rule of Britishers started as long back as in 1757 when, at the Battle of Plassey, forces of East India Company defeated Siraj-ud-Daula, the Nawab of Bengal. This struggle was the effervescence of discontent developed by Indians because of the attitude of the administrators of East India Company towards the nationals.

Established in seventeenth century, East India Company had its commercial interest only as its aim. It wanted a monopoly of the trade with India and the East, so that there could be no other English or European merchants or trading company to compete with it. The Company also did not want the Indian merchants to compete with it for the purchase in India or sale abroad of Indian products. The Company had, therefore, to wage long and fierce wars to achieve their aim. Since the trading areas were far away, across many seas, the Company had to maintain a powerful navy. It used its superior naval power to maintain its trading presence along the Indian coast and to drive out the Indian merchants from coastal and foreign trade.

The Company required large amounts of money to wage wars both in India and on the high seas. It needed money to maintain naval forces, army forts and trading posts in India. The money was raised through local taxation in its fortified towns like Calcutta (now, Kolkata), Madras (now, Chennai) and Bombay (now, Mumbai). Gradually, it became essential to expand its territories in India with a view to levy more taxes over larger areas and increase the Company's financial resources. To develop more and more it needed immense capital for investment in industries, trade and agriculture.

By 1750s and 1760s, Bengal and South India rapidly came under East India Company's political control. It acquired direct control over the State revenues of the conquered areas. It appropriated a large part of the wealth of local rulers, nobles and *zamindars* (landowners). From 1765 to 1770, the Company sent out of Bengal nearly thirty-three per cent of its revenue in the form of goods. The Company used its political power to acquire monopolistic control over Indian trade and production. The administrative structure of the Company was structured only to make the collection of revenue.

In the meantime, Britain had an Industrial Revolution. British industrialists needed foreign outlets for their ever-increasing output of manufactured goods. A vast and highly populated country, such as India, was a temptation to them. At the same time, British industries needed raw materials. Britain now wanted to exploit the Indian market and India had now to pay for the goods imported. The country also had to export a good deal of wealth to pay dividends to the Company's shareholders and pensions for British civil and military officials. These officials were also permitted to take their savings back home with them. The profits of British merchants and planters had also to be drained out of India. India was also required to pay interests and dividends on British capital invested in this country.

As a result of British rule, India was transformed by the end of the nineteenth century into a classic colony. It was a major market for British manufacturers, a big source of raw materials and foodstuffs, and an important field for the investment of British capital. Its agriculture was highly taxed for the benefit of imperial interests. The bulk of transport system, modern mines and industries, foreign trade, coastal and international shipping and banks and insurance companies were all under foreign control. India provided employment to thousands of middle-class Englishmen and nearly one-third of its revenues was spent in paying salaries to Englishmen. The Indian army was engaged in protecting and promoting British imperial interests in East, South East, Central and West Asia, North, East and South Africa.

When by 1760, Britain was developing into the leading developed and capitalist country of the world, India was being transformed into an underdeveloped country and a 'leading' backward, colonial country of the world. In fact, the two processes were interdependent in terms of cause and effect. The entire structure of economic relations between India and Britain, involving trade, finance and technology continuously developed India's colonial dependence and underdevelopment. The peasantry was perhaps the chief victim of British colonialism. The artisans and craftsmen had also suffered much at the hands of imperialism.

Against all this, though the Indian people resisted British rule in India from its very inception, their major struggle, as already stated, became manifest in 1757. Hardly a year passed till the 1857 rebellion when some part of the country or the other was not convulsed by armed rebellion. The continuous resistance, wholly traditional in character, took three broad forms: civil rebellions, tribal uprisings, and peasant movements.

Even the Indian soldiers serving in the British army were affected. Their discontent took the form of armed resistance led by the deposed chieftains of their descendants and relations, ex-soldiers and officials. Large sections of the peasantry and artisans joined these revolts, because of their own grievances and hardships. Extension of the British power to other parts of the country led to similar revolts. All the revolts and rebellions culminated in the Revolt of 1857 in which millions of peasants, artisans and soldiers participated.

The Revolt began at Meerut, thirty-six miles from Delhi, on 10 May 1857, with a mutiny of soldiers and then spread to Punjab in the north and Narmada to the south to Bihar in the east and Rajputana in the west. The Meerut soldiers killed their officers and set off for Delhi. Then soldiers in Delhi revolted, seized the city, and proclaimed the aged Bahadur Shah, as the Emperor of India. The soldiers thus transformed their mutiny into a revolutionary war. The mutiny of sepoys was followed by popular revolts of the civilian population. Over 1,50,000 people died. There was complete cooperation between Hindus and Muslims. The British Government mobilised its immense resources and suppressed the revolt most ruthlessly. Peasant unrest also broke out everywhere.

The second half of the nineteenth century witnessed the development of national political consciousness and the foundation and growth of an organised national movement. During this period, the modern Indian intelligentsia created political associations to spread political education and to initiate political work in the country. This work was to be based on new political ideas, a new intellectual perception of reality, new social, economic and political objectives, new forces of struggle and resistance and new techniques of political organisation. Raja Rammohan Roy was one of the first Indian leaders to start an agitation for political reforms. He fought for the freedom of the Press, trial by jury, the separation of the executive and the judiciary, appointment of Indians to higher offices, protection of the *ryots* from *zamindari* oppression, and development of Indian trade and industries. He based his entire public activity on the hope that a period of British rule would be followed by the emergence of a free India. He took keen interest in international affairs and supported the cause of liberty, democracy and nationalism.

The first political association to be started in India was the Landholders' Society at Calcutta in 1838. In 1843, the Bengal British Indian Society was organised with wider political objectives. In 1851, came the British Indian Association and the Madras Native Association. This followed Bombay Association in 1852. Many similar associations and clubs were established in smaller cities and towns all over the country. They presented political and economic demands before the British Indian government and the British Parliament. Their demand included the spread of education, association of Indians with the Government, larger employment of Indians in administrative services and the encouragement of Indian trade and industries. The failure of the Revolt of 1857 made it clear that the traditional political resistance to British rule under the leadership of the landed upper-classes could no longer succeed and that resistance to colonialism must flow along new channels. The younger elements became more active.

The politically conscious Indians increasingly felt the need for an all-India organisation to provide a common forum for the meeting of Indians and the formulation of a common programme of activity. The idea was given a more concrete shape by the Bombay group of nationalist political workers who cooperated with A.O. Hume, an Englishman and a retired Civil Servant, to bring together at Bombay in December 1885 political leaders from different parts of the country. These leaders decided to start the Indian National Congress to be presided over, in the first instance, by W.C. Banerjee. Hume's main purpose in encouraging the foundation of the Congress was to provide a 'safety valve' or a safe outlet to the growing discontent among the educated Indians. He wanted to prevent the union of a discontented nationalist intelligentsia with a discontented peasantry. Patriotic Indians cooperated with Hume because they did not want to arouse official hostility to their early political efforts and they hoped that a retired Civil Servant's active presence would allay official suspicions.

The nationalist leaders also took up the cause of Indian workers who had migrated to British colonies, such as South Africa, Malaya, Mauritius, Fiji, the West Indies, and British Guiana. These workers were being subjected to extreme measures of racial discrimination and other kinds of oppression in these countries. In many cases, they were being treated more like slaves. The nationalists gave full support to the popular struggle for human rights that was being waged in South Africa after 1893 by Mohandas Karamchand Gandhi. The Indian leaders also took up the cause of the plantation workers who were forced to live in conditions of near-slavery on low wages by the foreign planters.

It was the methods of political work of the early nationalists that earned them the title of Moderates. They believed that their main task was to educate people in modern politics, to arouse national political consciousness and to create a united public opinion on political questions. They held meetings where speeches of a very high political and intellectual calibre were made and resolutions setting forth popular demands were passed. Through the Press, the nationalists carried on a daily critique of the Government. These memorials and petitions were carefully drafted documents in which facts and arguments were diligently marshalled. Their second objective was to influence the British Government and British public opinion to introduce the desired changes. The basic weakness of the early nationalist movement lay in its narrow social base. The movement did not penetrate down to the masses. However, the early nationalists made a great advance in their political goals at the turn of the century. Their demand was no longer confined to petty reforms. They now demanded full self-government, including full Indian control over all legislations and finances. Dadabhai Naoroji was the first Indian to use the word *Swarajya* in Calcutta Session of the Congress in 1906.

The British authorities pushed further the policy of 'divide and rule' to counter the growing nationalist movement. They realised that the growing unity of the Indian people posed a major threat to their rule. The British authorities also followed a policy of apparent concessions on the one hand and ruthless repression on the other to put down the growth of nationalism. They believed that the spread of education had been a major cause of the growth of nationalism. Plans were now worked out to impose greater government control over it and to change its modern, liberal character. It was intended to be accomplished through the Education Act of 1903 and by keeping strict control over teachers through the system of government inspection of schools and colleges. Secondly, the Government decided to promote private colleges run by religious trusts. Modern secular education, which led to the spread of rational, democratic, and nationalist ideas, was sought to be replaced by a system based on religious and moral training.

In this way, the early nationalists could not achieve much practical success. The Government became more repressive. During the latter half of the nineteenth century, political consciousness of the people had been growing steadily. By the turn of the century, the general mood of discontent had spread to the rural gentry, the peasantry and the workers. The situation gave birth to a great number of new leaders who were more radical in their demands and who believed in a more militant form of nationalism. They were referred to as Extremists. While the main support for the moderate leaders had come from the intelligentsia and the urban middle-class, the new leaders, who emerged, appealed to a wider circle of the lower middle-classes, the students, and even a section of the workers and peasants. The early intellectual leadership was provided by persons like Rajnarain Bose and Bankim Chandra Chatterjee in Bengal and Vishnu Shastri Chiplunkar in Maharashtra. Bankim's hymn to motherland began with *Bandemataram*, which, later became a stirring call of patriotism and self-sacrifice. Bal Gangadhar Tilak was the first to advise peasants in Maharashtra to withhold payment of land revenues when their crops failed owing to drought or famine or pestilence. Lokmanya Tilak, Bipin Chandra Pal, Aurobindo Ghosh and Lala Lajpat Rai were the chief exponents of this militant school of nationalism. Rabindranath's *swadeshi* songs gave expression to the people's anguish and anger.

The militant nationalists added a glorious chapter to the history of the resurgence movement. They prepared the social base of the movement to include the lower middle-classes, students, youth and women. The partition of Bengal gave further momentum to the movement. In 1897, two brothers, Damodar and Balkrishna Chapekar of Poona (now, Pune) assassinated two British officers. Later, Aurobindo Ghosh planned some revolutionary activities. People took to bomb, pistol and individual acts of terrorism. They lost all faith in constitutional agitation or even in passive resistance. The British, they felt, must be overthrown by force. In Maharashtra, Nasik, Bombay and Poona became centres of bomb-manufacture. An attempt was made on Viceroy's life. Jackson, district Magistrate of Nasik, was shot at a farewell party. Some of the terrorist revolutionaries went abroad and established centres in Europe. They planned to obtain the help of countries, which were not friendly to Britain, or to collect arms and send them to their comrades in India secretly. Shyamji Krishna Varma, V.D. Savarkar and Lala Hardayal went to London. In Europe, Madam Cama and Ajit Singh were prominent.

Mahatma Gandhi's novel method of *Satyagraha* had yielded good results. The Congress stalwarts formed a high opinion of his character and his organising ability. Till his arrival in India from South Africa in 1915, he had not played any leading part in the Congress circles and was unknown to the masses. His austere habits and saintly grace, his use of Indian languages in preference to English and of religious text, made an impact on the people. His experiments in *Satyagraha* brought him into close touch with the masses. Hindu–Muslim unity, removal of untouchability and raising the status of women, were three causes very close to the heart of people. He believed that non-cooperation with evil is as much a duty as is cooperation with good.

The most important event in the struggle for freedom had been the massacre of Jalianwala Bagh on 13 April 1919. The people of the Punjab had been excited over war loans and the harsh methods of recruitment of Governor O'Dyer. The Muslims were deeply affected by the Khilafat propaganda. The government unnecessarily panicked and ordered the arrest of the principal leaders. The result was mob fury at Amritsar, where, following a police firing, some officials were killed and two British women seriously injured. Next day, General O'Dyer ordered his troops to open fire without warning on the unarmed crowd in a park from which there was no way out. Over 1,000 people died and several thousands were wounded. People were flogged in public and made to crawl where the two British women had been assaulted. Arrested persons were confined in cages. Hostages were taken; property was confiscated or destroyed; and Hindus and Muslims were hand-cuffed in pairs to demonstrate the consequences of unity. Martial law was proclaimed. Rabindranath Tagore renounced his knighthood in protest. The Punjab tragedy brought Mahatma Gandhi into the forefront of Indian politics. Many of the erstwhile moderate nationalists also now joined forces with Mahatma Gandhi.

On 31 December 1929, at midnight, which ushered the New Year, the Indian National Congress, under the Presidentship of Jawaharlal Nehru, pledged to achieve *Purna Swaraj*, total independence. A vast multitude of people saw Jawaharlal Nehru unfurl the tri-colour national flag on the banks of the Ravi and heard him proclaim that it was 'a crime against man and God to submit any longer' to British rule. Though fully committed to the ultimate objective of freedom, not all accepted the programme and methodology of the Congress. It was realised that terrorism had not succeeded in arousing the people to a national uprising for the overthrow of the British. With the elimination of most of the terrorists through execution or imprisonment, or their absorption in the Communist and other movements, revolutionary terrorism subsided. The Trade Union movement, too, had been crippled by repression. The official ban on the Communist Party was followed by Government ban in late 1934 on the Red Flag Trade Union Federation.

The direct executive authority of the Viceroy ruled British India. The rest of the country was made up of a large number of princely states, referred to by the British as Native States. These States of varying areas and population were ruled indirectly by the British through the Princes and Chiefs themselves. Most of the princes took care to see that their relationships with the British rulers were maintained with due submissive decorum. A few did not do this. This displeased the British authorities and they suffered the consequences, losing control over their States. The British Government had formed a purely consultative body of the princes called the Chamber of Princes (or Narendra Mandal) which was meant to standardise their relationship.

By 1935 Act, the British Government gave limited democracy to Indians. In the provinces, where the Congress ministries took office, the governments in the field of labour dispute, dissemination of primary education, etc., introduced several reforms. The Congress ministries in Madras initiated prohibition. The Madras Government also initiated a system of tripartite bargaining in labour disputes in which the Government provided conciliation machinery. It represented a liberal attempt to resolve labour disputes by the use of the collective bargaining method. It increased the political strength of the trade unions.

When the Second World War broke out on 3 September 1939 it placed the Indian leaders in a difficult situation. They were totally opposed to the Fascist philosophy. The Congress condemned Fascism and declared themselves openly in support of the suffering people of Spain, Ethiopia and Czechoslovakia. When, by the end of 1941, the war assumed a world conflagration, Britain became desperately anxious to have the full and active cooperation of India, not only to halt the Japanese advance but even the overall war effort. To secure this cooperation Britain felt that India had to be offered some firm promises for the future.

Accordingly, the British Government sent Sir Stafford Cripps, a member of the War Cabinet, to India with a Draft Declaration, which offered Dominion Status immediately at the end of the war, which also gave India the right of secession. To implement this proposal a Constituent Assembly would be set up as soon as hostilities ceased. The members of the Assembly were to be drawn from both British India and the

Native States. The Lower Houses of the Provincial Legislatures would elect Indian members. The rulers would nominate the representatives from the States. The British Government agreed to accept the Constitution framed by the Assembly and negotiate a treaty arrangement with India. Almost all the parties rejected this Declaration.

The failure of the Cripps Mission plunged the country in despondency and anger. It deprived the leaders from an opportunity to cooperate in full measure in the defence of the country. The Indian National Congress called upon Britain immediately to transfer the power to India. In August 1942, the All India Congress Committee passed resolution of 'Quit India'. Many leaders were arrested. Public life virtually came to standstill. Life was paralysed throughout the country. National songs and slogans, demanding the release of the leaders, rented the air. The situation was out of control. The students, workers and the peasants spearheaded the revolt. Ultimately, the Revolt of 1942 failed in the absence of a proper leader. However, the Revolt marked the culmination of the Indian Freedom Movement.

In April 1945, the war in Europe ended. British Prime Minister Churchill resigned. All the Indian leaders were released. Subhas Chandra Bose had already left India secretly in March 1941 to go to the Soviet Union and seek their help in India's struggle for freedom. He went to Germany and other countries. He raised Indian National Army. The war had completely changed the position and power of Britain in the world. The Soviet Union and the United States emerged as the big powers and both were in favour of Indian independence. Though Britain was victorious in the war, her economy and military strength had been seriously damaged. Her people, especially the defence personnel, were war weary. The Conservatives had been defeated in the fresh elections in Britain and the Labour Party, which had assumed office, was in favour of acceeding to the Indian demands. It was no longer possible for the British to continue in power. The fighting spirit of India had been aroused and if the nationalist demands were not adequately met the situation was expected to be explosive. Again, strikes and demonstrations increased all over British India touching the Princely States as well.

The British Government, therefore, decided to transfer power to India. They sent a Cabinet Mission to India. British Prime Minister, Clement Atlee, announced on 20 February 1947 that Britain would transfer power to India latest by June 1948. Lord Louis Mountbatten was sent to India as Viceroy to arrange for the transfer of power. India became free on 15 August 1947, but the country was partitioned. The western areas of the Punjab, the North West Frontier Province, Sind and Baluchistan in the west and the eastern half of Bengal and Sylhet district in Assam formed the new independent States of Pakistan. The pain and sadness of partition and its consequences diluted the pride and joy in the achievement of freedom.

However, we cannot gloss over the sacrifices made by many of our ancestors. Our Independence Day on 15 August every year, should continue to remind us how priceless it is for all of us. The ten essays included in this book bring to focus the travails and tribulations the freedom fighters encountered. Though such people are many but my purpose in introducing only a few of them is to present in this small and handy book only the glimpses of irrepressible feelings displayed by our people to ensure that the succeeding generations are able to live in peace and harmony.

In my efforts to present these essays, I have extracted information from various sources. I am indebted to authors of such books and library staff of Jamia Milia Islamia and

Delhi University Central Library for giving me an access to their books. My thanks are due to my wife, Mrs Asha Ahuja for allowing me to concentrate on this study after my office hours. My thanks are to Rupa & Company for undertaking publication of this book. I am also thankful to their dedicated team of editors and production specialists for endowing excellence to the presentation of this book. I do hope that with the efforts of this distinguished publishing house the book will be made available to the younger generation in various nooks and corners of the world to cherish the value of Independence bequeathed to us almost 58 years back.

5 January 2006   M.L. Ahuja

Lala Lajpat Rai

Lala Lajpat Rai was a great crusader to the cause of India's emancipation from the colonial rule of India. His words, 'every blow...drove a nail into the coffin of the Empire,' posed a challenge to the British Empire. Vaguely aware of his own approaching end, he said, 'And now, you, who have condemned me, I would fain prophesy to you; for I am about to die, and in the hour of death men are gifted with prophetic power. And I prophesy to you who have sentenced me to death, that immediately after my departure, punishment far heavier than you have inflicted on me will surely await you.' This was now left to the younger generation like Bhagat Singh to avenge his death. Bhagat Singh did not become popular because of his act of terrorism, but because he seemed to have vindicated the honour of Lala Lajpat Rai, and through him of the nation. He became a symbol, and within a few months each town and village of the Punjab resounded with his name. Innumerable songs grew up about him and the popularity that the man achieved was something amazing. Lala Lajpat Rai became immortal and a part of the struggle for India's freedom movement.

Lala Lajpat Rai was the first child of Munshi Radha Kishan, a teacher in the Government Middle School, Rupar in Ambala district. He was born on 28 January 1865. The child was born in Dhudike, a small village in the Moga tehsil of the Ferozepore district. When Lajpat grew up into a schoolboy he was more fond of books than of play. He became a constant victim of malaria, and acquired an enlarged spleen. Radha Kishan largely carried on the boy's schooling, first at home, where the lessons of the classroom were abundantly supplemented. The boy was intelligent and hardworking and a prize-winner as his father had been in his own day. His father taught him not merely reading, writing and arithmetic but soon made him interested in religion as well. The boy read parts of the *Quran* with his father and like him used to say his *namaz* and even observed the *Ramzan* fast, though occasionally.

In fact, his father was an orthodox Jain. His grandfather firmly believed in Islam though not a Muslim himself. His mother was in perpetual agony about her husband's inclination towards Islam but scrupulously became regular in her Sikh recitals. From his father, Lajpat inherited his fondness for the study of history, which, in fact, meant penchant for the epic in the widest possible sense. Radha Kishan taught the boy Firdaushi's immortal *Shahnama*, which is regarded as the Persian counterpart of Homer's epic or of Vyasa's *Mahabharata*. It created in the boy an appetite for more. The boy nurtured on this intellectual diet and sought after in books of history. But he did not neglect his schoolbooks. He regularly occupied the top position in his school. The Education Department granted him stipend. Before he was thirteen and while yet at the middle school, the boy was married to Radha Devi. He studied in the Mission High School at Ludhiana where, too, he was granted stipend as a promising boy. He passed his matriculation both from the University of the Punjab and Calcutta University, getting first class in the Calcutta University.

In February, at the age of sixteen, Lajpat joined the Government College. His first priority was to complete the law course and get a diploma that would enable him to earn a living. For his law examination he worked hard to qualify for *mukhtarship*. Frequent illness, the law-school priority, preoccupation with certain live issues in public life, and absorption in education of a type very different from the university curriculum, all combined in 1883 to keep his name out of the list of successful candidates in the intermediate arts examination. While in college, he came in contact with Guru Dutt, Hans Raj, Chetan Anand and Rai Shiv Nath who were instrumental in shaping his destiny.

In Punjab, the Arya Samaj placed great emphasis on the importance of Hindi and Sanskrit for Hindus. Lajpat Rai's friends at College, having definitely espoused the cause of Hindi and Sanskrit, beseeched him to discard Arabic in favour of Sanskrit. Lajpat left the study of Arabic and Persian. The Hindi movement soon found in him an active missionary. It was the beginning of Lajpat's public life. The first public speech that young Lajpat made was for the cause of Hindi at Ambala in 1882 when he was only eighteen. The magistrate present there reported this to the Principal of his college who advised Lajpat to concentrate only on his study. For some time, Lajpat was also attracted to Brahmo Samaj. But ultimately he continued to espouse the cause of Arya Samaj. He was soon in its inner counsel and became its leader. He addressed public meetings, raised funds and met the Arya fraternity in various cities. It was not the theological or doctrinal superiority of the Arya Samajic teaching that had attracted him. It had rather been the patriotic zeal of its members, their ambition of restoring *Aryavrata* to its ancient glory that inspired and permeated all activities sponsored by the Samaj and promoted by its members.

Guru Dutt, who lived a life of voluntary poverty, influenced Lajpat. The other person who influenced him was Hans Raj, for whom the Arya Samaj, as a progressive movement, was destined to play a vital part in the reorganisation of Hindu society. He had been drawn to the Samaj more by its patriotic than its philosophical or dogmatic side. Lajpat stood midway between the extremes of perfectionist idealism and of expediency, but his approach to problems interesting the Arya Samaj was much nearer that of Hans Raj than that of Guru Dutt. For him the supreme merit of the Samaj lay in its social, educational and welfare work, and in its stimulating a patriotic awareness in Hindu society. Lajpat intended to dedicate his life to the D.A.V. College like Hans Raj.

But poverty and the hardships of his parents made him realise the need for him to earn. Again, his priority was to be a *mukhtar* and to begin earning. He went to his small native town, Jagraon, to practise in the law courts as a *mukhtar*. He found both the profession and the town uncongenial. The place was too small for him. He felt choked in that little town where nobody thought of the big problems, where he could get no contacts, which would provide nourishment to his spirit. He was fed up with Jagraon and to at least improve things a little he shifted to Rohtak, where his father was now posted. He felt ashamed of being a mere *mukhtar*, and wanted to come into the higher hierarchy of law. And so he made an attempt at getting through the examination in 1883, but because of his preoccupation with so many other things he failed. He tried again and was now successful.

At Rohtak, he did some work in the local Arya Samaj and participated extensively in the activities of the Samaj and

D.A.V. College. He also wrote occasionally for the Press. He made some progress at the bar. In 1886, he accepted a somewhat important brief in the adjoining district of Hissar and finding that place more congenial settled down there. At Hissar, he was not merely a successful lawyer but, in many ways, a leading figure, particularly known for his hospitality.

When A.O. Hume started the Indian National Congress and Sir Syed Ahmad Khan opposed it in the name of the Muslim community, Lajpat saw playing Syed an unpatriotic role and wrote a series of 'Open Letters' which were printed anonymously. The letters were a creditable performance of a *mofussil* lawyer yet in his early twenties. He had made a promising beginning. He was known as the controversialist who had so effectively exposed no less an adversary than the great Sir Syed Ahmad Khan of Aligarh. He made two speeches at the Congress session, one of them being a sort of continuation of the Open Letters. This he delivered as the seconder of the principal resolution of the day, the one relating to the expansion of Legislative Councils by the introduction of an elective element. In this speech, he explained that Sir Syed, who was now seen as a leading opponent of the Congress, had formerly spoken in a different tone and thirty years earlier in his book on the 'mutiny' had himself made the same demand. Lajpat's speeches were greatly applauded. The 1888 session of the Congress threw Lajpat into a movement, which was directly political.

But more than the Congress, it was Lajpat's admiration for Mazzini that urged him towards the freedom movement. He had been introduced to the writings of the great Italian by Surendranath Banerjea's *Speeches of Joseph Mazzini* included in a collection of the Bengal orator's utterances which Lajpat happened to come across at the beginning of the nineteen 'eighties. The speeches made great impression on his tender heart. He read the life and teachings of Mazzini. The profound nationalism of the great Italian, his troubles and tribulations, his moral superiority, his broad human sympathies, enthralled him. Later, he translated the lives of Mazzini and that of Garibaldi in Urdu.

In 1883, Swami Dayananda Saraswati died. In the condolence meeting, Lajpat spoke for more than two hours and held the audience spellbound. It was this speech that made his reputation as a public speaker. He came to be regarded as the most effective orator of Arya Samaj. He now shifted to Lahore. The Arya Samaj had definitely struck root among the intelligentsia. Its activities expanded every year, both at Lahore and throughout the Punjab. It professed to revive the Vedic religion. It compared the ancient glories of India with her present degenerate condition. It thus fostered sentiments of patriotism. It wanted to equip the Hindu society for the struggle in the modern world. It wanted to eradicate child marriage, to abolish hereditary priesthood and simplify all rituals, lift the ban on the marriage of widows and on crossing the seas. The dynamic and progressive element among the Hindus rallied more and more round its banner. Politics during those days became the hobby of lawyers. The lawyers dominated in politics.

The Arya Samaj now became Lajpat's principal field of activity. Persons like Guru Dutt would not tolerate the smallest deviation from the doctrines laid down by Swami Dayanand. They maintained that the *Satyartha Prakasha* of Dayananda was true in every syllable. The more practical-minded people held that the *Satyartha Prakasha* curriculum was not meant for present-day conditions and that underlying it was the presumption of a Sanskrit-speaking *Aryavrata*. Lajpat found the cleavage becoming increasingly marked. He was rationalistic and valued intellectual independence too much to accept the 'infallibility' of the Swami or of anyone else. He had adopted Mazzini as his guru. He cast his lot with the group led by Hans Raj. At a meeting of Arya Samaj he said, 'Principles and not brick and stone constitute the Samaj. We joined the Samaj to reform our lives and to serve the people...' and thus he saved the Samaj from its split. He was chosen the first President of Arya Samaj.

After attending its Bombay session of the Indian Nation Congress in 1889 Lajpat Rai's enthusiasm towards the party abated a good deal. He did not attend its yearly Christmas gatherings. He wanted a constitution for the Congress to be drafted as he had done for the Arya Samaj but Hume did not find it convenient to accept the suggestion. He wrote a series of books in Urdu, which he named as the *Great Men of the World*. The first person he chose was Guisseppe Mazzini. That of Garibaldi followed it. Then were the biographies of Shivaji, Dayananda and Krishna. In his introduction to *Shivaji*, he explained why Hindus should pay heed not merely to the history of their past glory, but also to the history of their decline and how their turning a blind eye to this period had given scope to interested misrepresentation which had made current false notions about the Hindu mind and character. *Sri Krishna*, the last of this bunch of biographies, is well written. The Krishna of Lajpat Rai's story is mainly the Krishna of the *Mahabharata*.

Lajpat Rai was a pioneer among the Hindu leaders. Though he started the work under the Arya Samaj he soon addressed the entire Hindufold. He organised relief committees and raised funds during the great famines. The D.A.V. College placed a strong contingent of volunteers at his disposal. It was his foresight and his insistence that brought into being the premier Arya Samaj orphanage at Ferozepore of which he was the General Secretary for several years. The pressure of work was too much and it affected his health. He was now the father of three children—two sons and a daughter. But despite all this he continued to devote time to Arya Samaj and politics. In the beginning of the twentieth century, he agreed to accompany Gokhale to England.

For about a month in November 1905, Lajpat Rai toured English counties and Scotland, addressing meetings for the cause he represented. He addressed meetings in Manchester, Edinburgh, Liverpool and elsewhere. In an article on India and the British party politics, contributed to *The Punjabee*, Lajpat Rai wrote that there was nothing to choose between Liberals and Tories and the only people from whom some friendship might be expected were Labourites. Before returning to India, he made a brief trip to the United States. Back in Lahore, he received an unprecedented welcome. In his speech at the D.A.V. College, he foresaw 'blood raining down from the Indian sky. At the moment it was a seemingly a clear sky but tiny red specks were already visible.' One threatening 'unpleasant consequence' followed this soon after. Lahore had galvanised all of a sudden and became dangerous. The measure restricting the alienation of land evoked much hostility. Lajpat Rai and *The Punjabee* opposed the bill. At the next Congress session, a resolution was passed against this measure. Later on, when the Congress saw that a large body of Muslim landholders supported the measure as affording just protection to their rights, it dropped its opposition. The Punjab was in the grip of a whirlwind agrarian agitation.

In 1907, the wave of agitation swept virtually through the entire land. In Punjab, Ajit Singh, the '*Bharat Mata*' firebrand, like his brother Kishan Singh (father of Bhagat Singh) had been a student at the Anglo-Sanskrit School, Jullundur. The germs of patriotism among the two brothers were sown in this school through the leaders of Arya Samaj. Lajpat Rai knew Kishan Singh as a relief worker under him in the 1897 famine in the Central Provinces. Kishan Singh belonged to an extremist group and had been taking part in public debates. Lajpat Rai, as usual, was quite active in agitation. The British now felt convinced that Lajpat Rai was at the root cause of the agitation. Some of his friends suggested that he should leave Lahore and keep away till the storm had blown over. He was deported along with Ajit Singh, as leaders of the movement, under the provisions of Regulation III of 1818. He was taken to Diamond Harbour and from there to Burma. Both of them were released and returned back to Lahore after six months.

Back home, he was now a hero in politics. The sudden capture of Lajpat Rai, without trial, without charge and without notice, drove the young nationalists to frenzy. Even the sober and the thoughtful among them were in despair. All differences of opinion were forgotten and the whole country joined in protest. The extreme wing of the nationalists, however, decided to take the next step. They decided to use force and began to think of bomb and revolver and of guerilla warfare against the established despotism. In August 1908, he again went to England. By this time, Tilak was sentenced to six years' hard imprisonment and Aurobindo Ghose had been hauled up for writings in his paper. In England, he lectured widely. Amongst his new contacts in radical and revolutionary circles during this visit was his meeting with Kropotkin, the Russian anarchist Prince at that time who was considered among the foremost revolutionary writers and thinkers of Europe. He returned to India in March 1909.

He joined the Moderates' convention in the interest of unity. His attempt at reunion bore no fruit. There was a move that Hindus should have a separate organisation of their own.

The Punjab Hindu Sabha came into being. The first Hindu conference was held at Lahore in October 1909, i.e. shortly before the Congress could meet at Lahore. Lajpat Rai attended this conference as a delegate and made a speech on Hindu nationalism. His speech was full of quotations about ancient Hindu glory. He covered the ground from the religious angle, from the social angle and the new political context. In 1910, Bhai Parmanand, who was subsequently one of the Lahore conspirators and sentenced to transportation for life, was prosecuted under the Criminal Procedure Code. Bhai Parmanand was found in possession of a letter written by Lajpat Rai in 1907.

In 1910, Lajpat represented India at the Conference on Nationalities and Subject Races. Others from India who participated in the Conference were Bipin Chandra Pal, Dube and Sir Henry Cotton. The main Indian contribution was Lajpat Rai's speech on 'The Present Condition of India'. The greater part of the speech was devoted to the sad state of civil liberties, withdrawal of freedom of speech and the right of public meetings, barbarous punishments for political offences, complete gagging of the Press, and barbarous treatment of political prisoners, innovations in public and private espionage. After spending ten weeks in England, he made plans for a continental tour to France, Germany, Switzerland and Austria, Balkans and Turkey. But unusual situation developed. A formal declaration of war between Austria and Germany was declared. He contributed an anonymous article 'India and the War' in the *New Statesman*. On his way back to India, he visited America and Japan. He planned a regular sustained work for the cause of Indian freedom. The Indian Home Rule League of America was founded. He delivered lectures in various universities of Japan. He met Prime Minister Count Okuma, several cabinet ministers and other political personages, too.

A notable new contact for him was with D. Sun Yat Sen, the great Chinese leader, who, after the abortive second Chinese Revolution of July 1913, had taken refuge in Japan. To him the most wonderful thing, which he witnessed, was the intense patriotism of the Japanese and the progress they had made in every department of life within a short period.

The most important of Lajpat Rai's American bunch of books was *Young India*. It provides an interpretation of the Indian Nationalist movement from within, inside the Congress and without it, and writer's detached non-party attitude combined with the deep thought and objective scrutiny to which he had subjected the Indian problem. Strict adherence to constitutionalism, passive resistance, the terrorists' bomb and revolver, and attempts at an armed rising are all interpreted from the different angles of their respective votaries and then subjected to a cold and objective scrutiny with the searchlight of criticism in hand in a masterly way that remains unequalled. After some time, he started a monthly journal, and named it *Young India*. The book was banned. But, in England, an English edition was printed under the guidance of Commander Josiash C. Wedgwood. He challenged the police from the floor of the House of Commons to do their worst. A 'companion volume' to *Young India* followed it. It bore an eye catching title, *England's Debt to India*. Lajpat Rai's next book on the political situation was published in 1919 and was called *The Political Future of India*. While in America, Lajpat Rai also gave his American readers several pamphlets. He also wrote his Autobiography in Urdu during his stay in America.

Lajpat Rai was elected President of the Congress in July 1920 and he presided over its session in Calcutta (now, Kolkata). In his presidential address, he surveyed for his audience the entire O'Dyer tenure to show that 'it was all only through a regime of terror and fright and that it culminated to its logical conclusion in the months of April and May 1919.' He drew up a regular chargesheet against General Dyer charging him with deliberately intensifying the 'divide-and-rule' policy and fomenting communal and rural–urban dissension, with having used his authority in illegal ways in the interest of his campaigns for recruitment and war funds.' He marshalled his evidence in support of the charges he made. Back in Lahore he quietly settled down to the work he had taken in hand before the non-cooperation session. He worked for his Urdu daily, the *Bandemataram*. When non-cooperation was launched, at a Special Congress at Calcutta, he said that he was opposed to that item of non-cooperation, which related to the boycott of schools and colleges. He addressed a public meeting at Lahore and told the students and others that he would welcome the abolition of all the arts and law colleges.

He was arrested at the Punjab Congress meeting on 20 February 1922, when the Congress resolved to launch a campaign of civil disobedience. He spoke of his imprisonment as 'moral *sadhana*' and thanked God for this opportunity. While in prison, he wrote some books and a number of articles. He was in the prison for two years and this affected his health. He was not able to digest the prison diet, his insomnia got worse and he developed dyspepsia. A low fever attacked him. The fever persisted. His lung condition became a source of deep concern. He was released on 16 August 1923.

In spite of his failing health, Lajpat Rai kept playing active role in politics and towards the cause of Servants of India Society. The Congress leaders found it expedient to send him to England again. It was a trip undertaken primarily for his health. There, he met Prime Minister Ramsay MacDonald and his old friends. Motilal Nehru kept him abreast with the developments. Lajpat Rai was invited to preside over a Hindu Conference in Burma. There, he met his old Burmese friends, and made new contacts among them. He met the Indian settlers there. From Burma he returned to New Delhi to attend the Assembly session. A few days later, he formally joined the Swaraj Party. In 1920, he was actively involved in the Indian trade union movement. As workers' delegate, he participated in the International Labour Conference, which started on 26 May 1926. There, he met Rousseau, Mazzini, Kropotkin, Lenin, Romain Rolland, and others. Later, as he thought that 'non-cooperation' could not, at that stage, suit the working class, he resigned his AITUC office, which he held as national executive.

As an ardent nationalist, Lala Lajpat Rai, who, by now, had endeared himself to the masses, had not abjured his duties towards the Hindu community, mainly of the nature of social reform or of uplift of backward sections. Whenever the Hindus faced a calamity, man-made or act of God, they expected Lalaji and Malaviyaji to rush to their help. Because of these activities Lalaji was dubbed by some as a 'communalist'. The only 'communal' item that figured in Lalaji's activity was his association with the Hindu Mahasabha. He supported the Muslims in their Khilafat demand wholeheartedly. He always strove after a concrete and well-defined settlement based on considerations of equity and of mutual accommodation by Hindus and Muslims. He remained consistent in his attitude towards the Hindu–Muslim issue. He made an earnest, detailed, realistic study of the Hindu–Muslim dissension in a series of thirteen articles, which he wrote in 1924 for the Press. He worked closely with M.A. Jinnah during the pre-non-cooperation days.

The last session of the Congress that Lala Lajpat Rai could attend was the fortieth at Allahabad. The first one he had attended was the fourth at Allahabad. His work was very strenuous. He had been able to get no rest since his return from Europe. He wanted to have rest and set sail for Europe on 4 May 1927. This time, he eschewed political work. On his return, he finished his last book, *Unhappy India*. It was published in 1928. Simon Commission landed for the second time on 11 October 1928. On 27th and 28th he presided at Etawah over the deliberations of the Agra Provincial Hindu Conference. He had gone there to mobilise Hindu opinion in favour of the Nehru report proposals, the Nehru scheme and the Simon boycott. He led a huge procession 'Go back, Simon'. It was the most orderly and the best controlled demonstration. The police used *lathi* (cane) charge to disperse the crowd. *Lathis* rained on Lala Lajpat Rai. But he was dauntless. He did not permit the people to hit back. He himself took the blows and shouted with a lion's roar at his assailant. The assailant was Scott, the Senior Superintendent of Police. When the assault had halted, Lala Lajpat Rai addressed a mammoth public meeting. He said, 'Every blow that they hurled at us drove one more nail into the coffin of the Empire.' He said if he died and if the young men whom he had kept under check decided on a contrary course of action his spirit would only bless whatever they thought fit to do. Lala Lajpat Rai resumed his work serving his people. However, on 17 November 1928, he left his mundane existence leaving his countrymen to take up the unfinished task.

Lalaji's prophecy, it seemed, was fulfilled. His accusers were universally despised and shamed. They were Scott, the Senior Superintendent of Police, and Saunders, the assistant. Scott was sent away from his Lahore job. Lads, who perhaps really wanted Scott rather than Saunders, had died on the spot, shot at by one of his younger men. Later, it was left to Bhagat Singh and his associates to avenge the assault on Lalaji. The assault on Lalaji became a national humiliation. The young generation became restless. Young Bhagat Singh had inherited a rich family legacy. His father, Kishan Singh, had started life as a social-worker under Lajpat Rai's direction. A far more potent influence had been his, uncle Ajit Singh. Bhagat Singh seemed destined for the martyr's role. The assault on the people's leader and the extreme national humiliation involved therein acted as the stimulus for the inmost secret to come out and announce itself from the scaffold. The stimulus was a statement by Basant Devi who, as a 'Woman of India' demanded from India's youth a befitting reply to the affront to the nation. The youth of India could ill-afford to ignore such a challenge. The reply came through Bhagat Singh, who seemed to have been haunted by the challenge.

Gopal Krishna Gokhale

Gopal Krishna Gokhale had been the founding member of Indian National Congress, a great patriot and a freedom fighter. As a leading legislator of the time he combined three unusual qualities: incisive analysis, felicitous expression and a manner wholly removed from ostentation. Whatever he said bore the impress of earnestness and was the expression of his innate feelings to seek the welfare of the downtrodden masses. Mahatma Gandhi called himself the disciple of Gokhale. He said, 'Mr Gokhale taught me that the dream of every Indian, who claims to love his country, should be not to glorify in language but to spiritualise the political life of the country. He inspired my life...' He called Gokhale a saintly politician. Gokhale had many virtues. The chief amongst them was his complete dedication at a very young age to the service of the country, with selfless devotion. He was more than a statesman and was essentially a creative genius. His oratory was a work of art in words, but he was not only artistic in words but an artist in works and conceptions. He had a balanced intellect and studied both sides of the subject too well to take extreme views.

Gopal Krishna Gokhale was born on 9 May 1866 in a village called Kotluk in Ratnagiri district of the old Bombay Presidency. He belonged to a middle-class Chitpavan Brahmin family. His father, Krishnarao worked as a clerk and later as sub-inspector of police in Kagal, a small feudatory state of Kolhapur State. Krishnarao's wife was not educated but she was a religious lady. The couple had two sons and four daughters.

Gopal had his elementary education at home. He was sent to Kolhapur along with his brother for further studies some time during 1874–75. He was hardly thirteen when his father expired. Gopal's uncle, Antaji, took care of the family. The family was now faced with financial hardship. Gopal was conscious of the sufferings of his family and spent each fraction of the money given to him for study with utmost care. At times, he studied under the street lamp with a view to save on the cost of kerosene. He passed his matriculation examination at the age of fifteen.

Gopal was married at the age of fourteen. His wife suffered from leucoderma. With her consent he married again. The second wife died in 1900 when Gopal was barely thirty-four. He had a son who died early and two daughters.

Gopal was a keen sportsman. He regularly played cricket from 1887 to 1889. He played tennis and billiards off and on. Once he defeated an English opponent at billiards on a voyage from England to India. He loved cards and chess, too.

Amidst extreme poverty, Gopal didn't think it proper to be of further burden to his elder brother by pursuing his study in college. But his brother, Govind, insisted that Gopal should continue his education. Govind's wife sold her ornaments for Gopal to join Rajaram College at Kolhapur in January 1882. Gopal passed his Previous examination, as it was then called, in 1882. For the second year, he joined the Deccan College at Poona, his stay in this college was short as he rejoined the

Rajaram College and soon started the second year's course. He did his final year from the Elphistone College in Bombay (now, Mumbai). He took mathematics as his optional subject and secured second class in 1884.

In 1882, the editors of two weeklies, *Kesari* in Marathi and *Mahratta* in English, were arrested for publishing some letters. In sympathy with the editors the public raised some funds. The New English School and the Deccan College also raised funds. The students of Rajaram College staged a play, Shakespeare's *Comedy of Errors*, to raise funds. Young Gopal played the role of abbess in the play. This was Gopal's first initiative towards the political cause. He had his B.A degree in 1884 at the age of eighteen.

Gopal Krishna Gokhale was appointed teacher first in Poona and then in Ratnagiri. He devoted his spare time for the study of law. For that purpose he joined the Law College in Bombay (now Mumbai) where he had to go every weekend. Though he cherished the desire to be a lawyer, circumstances did not allow him to pursue law studies much longer. In 1885, he delivered his first public lecture at Kolhapur. The subject was 'India Under the British Rule'. He captivated the audience with his eloquence in the English language. Later, he joined the Ferguson College where he taught Southey's *Life of Nelson*. Tilak taught mathematics in this college and both became friends. He developed the habit of committing to memory the writings of the best authors. Among the literary masterpieces memorised by him were Milton's *Paradise Lost* and the speeches of Burke, Gladstone, John Bright and several other British orators and parliamentarians. While he studied literature and liberalism mainly to improve his scholarship and power of analysis, they stood him in good stead later in his career as legislator and statesman. In course of time, he had differences with Tilak.

After the exit of Tilak from the Ferguson College, Gokhale began to take classes in mathematics. Later, he taught economics and history as well. He was quite methodical and took pains to explain all the allusions, especially the historical references. He contributed some articles to the *Mahratta*. When Agarkar started a periodical, *Sudharak*, Gokhale was in charge of its English side. In 1886–87, he wrote a series of articles in the *Mahratta* about 'General War in Europe.'

Gokhale became a teacher in the Deccan College when he was barely nineteen. In 1895, Gokhale became a seniormost member of the Deccan Education Society. He was offered the post of Principal in Fergusson College but he declined it. He was Secretary of the Deccan Education Society for some years. As Secretary, at times, he had to face a difficult situation, but his persuasive demeanour, engaging manners, and burning desire to conduct the institution served him well in serving the cause of Fergusson College. He was also a member of the University Senate for a number of years and took great interest in its deliberations.

He came in contact with Ranade when both Gokhale and Ranade were teachers in Fergusson College. Ranade was one of the founders of Indian National Congress and rose to be a High Court Judge. In politics, Ranade was an uncompromising constitutionalist. He was as interested in economics as in political reform. From 1887 to 1892, Gokhale took lessons from Ranade, who was a hard taskmaster indeed. Ranade's method of work included the study of every important piece of paper published by the government. He would then write his own scholarly and powerful manner his reactions to government policies and communicate them to the government. Those were the days when politics had not been declared out of bounds for civil servants. Ranade wanted the Indian public to be educated in the art of government.

Gokhale learnt from Ranade many things. This laid the basis of his entire public life. He learnt from his master how knowledge was to be combined with faith and fortitude to serve the people and how accurate figures were essential in dealing with intricate problems and how intensity of thought was more essential than language—all this and more Gokhale learnt from the master. But he was not concerned with the religious and social views of his master. Ranade's influence enabled Gokhale to make his choice for life.

Gokhale began his political career as the Secretary of Sarvajanik Sabha. He started the work under the supervision of Ranade. Before the advent of the Indian National Congress, there was no all-India institution in the country to ventilate the grievances of the people. But in the three metropolitan cities of Calcutta, Bombay and Madras (now Kolkata, Mumbai, and Chennai, respectively) there were organisations, which performed that function. In Bombay, Dadabhai Naoroji established the Bombay Association in 1853. Fourteen years later, a similar institution was started at Poona (now Pune). At first called Poona Association, it changed its name three years later and came to be called the Sarvajanik Sabha. The object of the Sabha was to bring the needs and feelings of the people to the attention of the government. It was an intermediary between the rulers and the ruled. Gokhale edited Sabha's quarterly journal. He also contributed articles in it. However, in 1896, Gokhale left the Sarvajanik Sabha and became the Secretary of newly floated Deccan Sabha. He went to England on behalf of the Sabha to present the Indian case before the Welby Commission.

The Welby Commission was appointed 'to inquire into the administration and management of the military and civil expenditure incurred under the authority of the Secretary of State for India-in-Council or the Government of India.' It was entrusted with the task of apportioning the charges between the Governments of India and Britain. Earlier, there had been a great dissatisfaction in India that her revenues were diverted for conquering territories beyond India's borders, that the Exchange Compensation Allowances given to servants recruited in Europe were unjustified, that the civil services were manned by Englishmen, that the European traders were given such concessions as to lead to exploitation, that public works engineers had launched an agitation for increase of salaries, and that the new railway lines undertaken for construction were for giving facilities to the foreigners for exploiting untapped resources in India.

Gokhale took great pains to bring to light all these facts. To him the voting on Budgets was a way of guarding Indian interests. He stated that a large European army was maintained on a war footing at a time of peace and that India was paying high salaries to these Europeans. One of the notable things mentioned by him in his written evidence related to the remarks of the Finance Committee appointed in 1886 of which Ranade was a member. The favour shown to European traders and commercial interests was another point established before the Commission. He stressed that the imported goods were killing indigenous industries and throwing artisans and small craftsmen back on to the land. He was subjected to tough examination. The attempt to make him admit that his contentions were wrong failed. He made several suggestions to the Commission for improving the Indian budgets. He wanted the budgets to be passed item by item in the Supreme Legislative Council.

In 1889, A.O. Hume wanted fifty good men and true of unselfishness, moral courage and self-control, men imbued with the active spirit of service to dedicate their lives to establishing a democratic government of India. Gokhale could be counted as one amongst them. At the age of twenty-seven, Gokhale came to be recognised as a leader of the Congress. He attended almost all the Congress sessions till the end of his life except in 1903 and 1914 when he was ill. He took an active part in the deliberations of the Congress and used to speak on the resolutions before it when called upon to do so. His power of expression, his intimate knowledge of the subject under consideration and his manner of developing an argument created an excellent impression on the leaders of the Congress.

In 1899, Gokhale won the election to the Bombay Legislative Council. He took special interest in three important problems in the Council: the Famine Code, the Land Alienation Bill, and the working of municipalities. On 30 May 1901, the Bombay Government introduced a Land Alienation Bill in the Council. Gokhale studied the problem of indebtedness of the peasantry thoroughly and his arguments were irrefutable. He suggested that this piece of legislation should be postponed and a comprehensive inquiry made into the whole question. He proved that poverty and indebtedness had increased under British rule. His ability in marshalling facts, rebutting official arguments, pressing home his point of view and making constructive suggestions came in for praise. As a legislator, he combined three unusual qualities: incisive analysis, felicitous expression and a manner wholly removed from ostentation. He never sought to score a skilful point. Whatever he said bore the impress of earnestness, and arose from the inner urge to seek the welfare of the downtrodden masses. His words gave expression to what his heart felt. His advocacy of prohibition, as of the cause of famine sufferers, sprang from his solicitude for the welfare of the people.

Between 1902 and 1911, Gokhale made eleven speeches on the Budget and thirty-six other important speeches.

Amongst the subjects, which he spoke on, were the Official Secrets Act, the Indian Universities Act, the Cooperative Credit Societies Act, the Seditious Meetings Act, the Press Bill, reduction or avoidance of debt, Railway finance, increase in public expenditure, the cotton excise duties, import duty on sugar, the public services, the taxable minimum income, the Civil Marriage Bill, indentured labour, the cost of building New Delhi, surpluses and reserves, gold currency, and the Elementary Education Bill. These speeches bear the imprint of his indefatigable study, a liberal outlook and an abiding interest in every thing that would advance the interests of the country. The subjects that he pointedly dealt with in his budget speeches were the salt duty, Army expenditure, currency surpluses, the Indianisation of services and taxation. In his fight against the bureaucracy, his approach was constitutional. His endeavour was to build his case on facts and logic and through persuasion to bring about a change of heart in those who counted. He was the most active member of the Imperial Legislative Council. Many of his colleagues called him the Leader of the Opposition.

Gokhale believed in the development of education as means of raising the country. The Government felt that universities and colleges had become hotbeds of seditious teaching and had to be brought under control completely. There was a growing dissatisfaction among the educated classes. Even those who secured high degrees were not getting the same salaries and the same posts as the Europeans brought from abroad. Many qualified persons did not even secure employment. As a result, some of them nurtured revolutionary ideas. Gokhakle opposed the Bill. He stated that the effect of the Act would be to dissociate the Indian element from university administration and place it in the hands of European professors. He made several constructive suggestions to improve the state of affairs. He wanted the percentage of children attending schools to be quadrupled. Expenditure incurred on education had to grow fourfold. He suggested that two-thirds of this amount should be borne by the Government and the rest by the local bodies. He wanted education to be made compulsory for boys between six and ten years.

Gokhale believed that the country needed a selfless and intelligent band of workers to dedicate their lives to the service of the country. Indians had yet to take to politics with the requisite knowledge and study of problems. The spirit of service was still to grow. This was particularly true in the field of politics. The need for public work based on an ardent devotion to the uplift of the downtrodden had gradually come to be recognised. The Deccan Education Society and certain other institutions of Poona sprang from this zeal. Servants of India Society was founded towards this end in view on 12 June 1905 by Gokhale's colleague Shivaram Hari Sathe. Gokhale was the first to be administered oath for the development of the country. The Society aimed at spiritualising politics. The Society's constitution enjoined that love of the country must so fill the heart that all else should appear as of little consequence. The Society was meant to be a sort of post-graduate institution where members under training had to study hard the issues of the day, come into contact with the people, succour the afflicted, and fight against foreign rule in a constitutional way. The Society has branches at Bombay, Nagpur, Madras and Allahabad apart from the central office at Poona. The spacious building that houses the central office is now the Gokhale School of Politics and Economics.

Gokhale and Lajpat Rai went to England on 16 September 1905, a few months after the Servants of India Society had been founded. As a powerful orator, Lajpat Rai addressed mass meetings, while Gokhale addressed meetings of Parliamentarians, Liberals and selected sections of the people. The Congress was thinking of boycotting British textiles. Gokhale wanted this to be understood not only by the general public but also by the workers of Manchester and Lancashire. He told the workers at Manchester that they had every right to be angry not with India, which was wronged, but with those who had committed the wrong of partitioning Bengal. The Indian people, grown desperate, could not retaliate in any other way than by refusing to buy British goods. Gokhale had a taxing time working for almost eighteen hours a day. The strain was so great that he had to undergo an operation of the throat on board the steamer on his return journey. He returned to India on 5 December 1905.

Gokhale became the President of Indian National Congress at a time when partition of Bengal by Lord Curzon had awakened the slumbering nationalism in India. The militant spirit shown by Bengal against British rule provoked Curzon. Gokhale's presidential address at the Benaras session was forceful and informative. He made a survey of the regime of Lord Curzon. He compared his rule to the rule of Aurangzeb. Both regimes were excessively centralised and intensely personal. Lord Curzon was great in many ways, but he could not understand the people of India, as he did not possess a sympathetic imagination. He dealt with the Swadeshi and boycott movements.

Like Mahatma Gandhi, Gokhale believed in persuasive methods for bringing about a change of heart, but unlike Mahatma Gandhi he did not resort to direct action. He was, by conviction, a moderate and a liberal. Nothing could make him swerve from the position he had taken up. He knew that there were two forces at work in the country: unwillingness on the part of the government to move with the times and impatience on the part of the extremists. But he would oblige neither group. His consolation lay in being true to himself and to the cause, which he so sincerely advocated. His position was unenviable. He went to England for the fourth time in 1908 on behalf of the Bombay Presidency Association for pleading, arguing with, and persuading Lord Morley before the Indian Reforms Act of 1909 was introduced. He laboured hard for the sake of the country but success was not to be his at that time.

There was a split between the moderates and extremists in the Congress at its Surat session. Gokhale played the role of a mediator. In the Congress session held at Lahore, Gokhale moved a resolution on South Africa. Mahatma Gandhi was glad to read this stirring exposition of passive resistance from Gokhale, whom he had already enshrined in his heart as his master. He praised Mahatma Gandhi for leading an austerely simple life devoting all the highest principles of love to his fellow-beings, to truth and justice. His speech had a magical effect. Mahatma Gandhi was given a standing ovation. Gold and currency notes were showered on him to aid the struggle in South Africa. Mahatma Gandhi wrote to Gokhale giving detailed accounts of how the sums were spent and about the progress of the struggle. At the invitation of Mahatma Gandhi, Gokhale reached Capetown on 22 October 1912. The Union Government in South Africa received him cordially and placed a saloon at his disposal. Mahatma Gandhi provided him all kinds of facilities. Gokhale won the hearts of the Europeans by his sincere and eloquent speeches, full of humility, warmth and love. He went to Johannesburg, Natal and Pretoria. He left South Africa on 17 November. But after Gokhale left, the old order continued. In Bombay, Gokhale was criticised for the compromise he had entered into in South Africa.

When Gokhale was in England for the seventh time to participate in the meetings of the Public Service Commission, his health deteriorated. He met Mahatma Gandhi in Poona and wanted him to join the Servants of India Society. He asked his colleague to open an account for Gandhiji in the Society's books and give him whatever he might require for the expenses of the *ashram* and for his public work. It was this unbounded love that made Gandhiji say that Gokhale was like the Ganges. He breathed his last on 17 February 1915. Soon after he visited Poona, Gandhiji went to Santiniketan. It was there that he received news of Gokhale's death. He had come to regard Gokhale his mentor. Gokhale, indeed, was more than a guru to him. He was as a father and mother to him. At a condolence meeting, Gandhiji gave expression to his grief and said, 'I set out to find a true hero and I found only one in the whole of India. That hero was Gokhale.' As a sign of mourning he decided to go barefoot for a year. He hurried back to Poona on 22 February. He was now determined to join the Society. While Gokhale was there, he told himself, he did not have to seek admission as a member. Now it was his duty to do so. Messages of condolence poured in from all over the world and meetings were held to express grief. The bust of Gokhale in Parliament's library and the Gokhale School of Politics and Economics on the premises of the Servants of India Society would continue to remind the values Gopal Krishna Gokhale cherished during his lifetime.

Mahatma Gandhi

'...a glory has departed and the sun that warmed and brightened our lives has set and we shiver in the cold and dark ... that man with the divine fire changed us also ... we have been moulded by him during these years; and out of this divine fire, many of us also took, a small spark which strengthened and made us work to some extent on the lines that he fashioned...'

Thus spoke Pt. Jawaharlal Nehru on the death of Mahatma Gandhi, Father of the Nation, who was, in the words of Dr S. Radhakrishnan, 'a giant among us, measured by the greatness of his soul.'

Mohandas Karamchand Gandhi, whom the world called *Mahatma* or 'Great Soul', was born on 2 October 1869 at Porbandar, a small town on the western coast of India. His father, Karamchand Gandhi, Dewan of Porbandar, was a truthful, courageous, and intelligent person with a stern character. His mother, Putlibai, was a religious, gentle soul who left a deep impression on the mind of her son who worshipped her.

As a child Mohan went to an elementary school in Porbandar where he was a 'mediocre student', extremely shy,

timid and averse to games. At school he met Sheikh Mahtab
whose athletic build and physique fascinated Mohan who
himself was of a comparatively slight build and was scared
of ghosts, thieves and snakes. Mahtab convinced Mohan that
'the mighty Englishman' was able to rule over the 'puny
Indian' because the Englishman derived his 'Herculean'
strength from animal flesh. So, Mohan who came from an
orthodox vegetarian family tasted cooked meat clandestinely.
This was his first experiment in patriotism, but it proved too
weighty a burden on his conscience.

At the age of thirteen, while still at school, Mohan was
married to Kasturba, also thirteen. His father died in 1885
when he was just sixteen. Two years later, he matriculated
and entered a college in the nearby state of Bhavnagar since
there were no colleges in Rajkot. He found studies tedious,
the English medium difficult and the atmosphere uncongenial.
A friend of the family suggested that if he hoped to take his
father's place in the state service he had better become a
barrister in England. Mohan jumped at the idea and began
raising money to study in England. His mother, however, was
unwilling to part with her darling boy and expose him to all
sorts of temptations. In order to reassure Mohan took a vow
not to touch wine, woman and meat and sailed for England
on 4 September 1888. The glamour of English life
overwhelmed him during the early period of his stay. He got
new clothes made, bought a silk hat, spent ten pounds on an
evening dress made in Bond Street and flaunted a double
watch-chain of gold. He took lessons in elocution and French
and spent three guineas to learn ballroom dancing. He was
introduced to the theosophical thought of Madame Blavatsky
and Annie Besant. It was through them that he came to know
of the *Bhagavad Gita* in Edwin Arnold's English rendering
which opened for him 'a new view of life'.

Later, in Johannesburg he found the company of Theosophists congenial. Their interest in Hindu sciptures and, in particular, *Bhagavad Gita* stimulated him to turn to his own religion for a deeper source of strength.

After three years, and having been called to the bar and enrolment in the High Court on 11 June 1891, the young barrister sailed home. His sojourn in England had been both profitable and stimulating. In India, he came to know that his mother had passed away in his absence. Since there was little scope for making a fortune from legal practice at Rajkot, he came to Bombay, (now Mumbai), to practise law. He was engaged to defend a petty suit in a Small Causes Court. As he rose to cross-examine the plaintiff's witness, he became nervous. He sat down in confusion and returned the fees to the client's agent. He never went to court again and sought a part-time job as an English teacher instead. When the Principal found that the candidate did not have a university degree in teaching, 'he regretfully refused' him.

After a luckless trial of six months in Bombay, Mohan wound up his small establishment and returned to Rajkot where, with the help of his brother and other contacts, he was able to earn a modest income by drafting petitions and memorials. At this juncture, a Muslim firm of Kathiawar, which had large business interests in South Africa, offered to send him there for one year to assist their counsel in a big law-suit. Mohan readily accepted the offer and sailed for Durban in April 1893.

Once in Durban, Mohandas found that though the British and Dutch together were a small minority in Natal, they treated both native Africans and Indians as less than human. Indians, who had been originally brought in 1860 at the request of the European settlers to help build their plantation economy, had been lured as indentured labourers on a five-year contract with the right to stay on as free residents on their own. Merchants and traders also followed the native negro mainly because they found them more industrious and competitive to the whites.

Mohan encountered the first humiliating experience in South Africa when a white passenger boarding the train, objected to the presence of a 'coloured man' in the compartment. He was ordered by a railway official to shift to the 'van compartment'. On Mohan's refusal to do so, a constable pushed him out. It was winter and bitterly cold. Mohan's overcoat was taken away with the luggage and he lacked the courage to ask for it. So, he sat in the dark waiting-room, shivering the whole night, thinking, 'Should I stand up for my rights or should I go back to India?' Again, while travelling from Charlestown to Johannesburg, Mohan was asked by the white conductor, to sit on a dirty sack-cloth on the footboard. When Mohan refused, the conductor rained blows on him while Mohan clung desperately to the brass rails.

Having seen for himself the plight of his countrymen in that country, Gandhi, on reaching Pretoria, addressed a meeting of the Indian community. It was the first public demonstration of his art as a speaker at which, later he became adept. He advised the audience to organise themselves into an association and to meet regularly to discuss their problems, to formulate and represent the grievances of their community. Gandhi guided the Indian community to resist the bill to disfranchise Indians. A petition was drafted and sent to the Prime Minister, the Speaker, the British Secretary of the State for Colonies, and other important members of the government. *The London Times* upheld the Indian claim as valid, and for the first time people in India were made aware of the hardships and ignominy of their countrymen in South Africa.

Gandhi got himself enrolled as an advocate of the Supreme Court of Natal. An organisation, known as the Natal Indian Congress, was formed and became an effective instrument to rouse the conscience not only of Indians but also of the liberal elements in England. After a brief stay in India, Gandhi returned to South Africa. Once when an English barber declined to cut his hair he did not take offence but started cutting it himself. Thus, self-help became the basic tenet of his social philosophy. This was the first step in his evolution as the *Mahatma*.

In 1903, Gandhi started a weekly, known as *Indian Opinion*, in four languages—English, Gujarati, Hindi and Tamil. In 1904, the Indian community in Johannesburg was afflicted by a sudden outbreak of plague. As soon as Gandhi came to know of it, he rushed to the aid of the victims with Dr Godfrey. In this process, he also came in contact with Albert West and Henry Polak. It was Polak who introduced him to Ruskin's *Unto the Last* which had profound influence on him.

In May 1919, accompanied by a delegation, Gandhi visited London where the prospective Union of the South African colonies was being considered by the British Parliament. He interacted with the politicians and the Press and pleaded for justice to the Indians. There he also met the revolutionary-minded Indians like Madan Lal Dhingra. True patriotism, according to l him, 'means the welfare of the whole people, and if I could secure it at the hands of the English I should bow down my head to them.' Back in South Africa, Gandhi started his civil resistance movement.

When Gandhi returned to India, he was a transformed personality. Gone was the timid and shy boy afraid of voicing his own feelings. He now emerged as a man with an iron will. By this time, Gokhale, Tilak and other famous leaders had roused the people of India to voice their feelings of discontent against the British. Gandhi discerned his simmering discontent of the Indian masses against the Raj. He started participating in the Congrsess Party's sessions and in 1917, he launched an agitation in Champaran, a small town in Bihar, full of indigo plantations. There, the tenants were bound by law to plant three out of every twenty parts of the land with indigo for the landlord. This system was known as the *Tinkathia* system, as three 'kathias' out of twenty (which make one acre) had to be planted with indigo.

When the British Indian Government passed the Rowlatt Act (1919), its recommendations startled Gandhi, and he formed a *Satyagraha Sabha* with the help of Sardar Vallabh Bhai Patel, Sarojini Naidu and others. A general *hartal* and *satyagraha* were observed in April 1919. A peaceful meeting held at Jallianwala Bagh, Amritsar, to protest against the Rowlatt Act, was fired upon mercilessly, without any warning, on the orders of General Dyer. Hundreds of innocent persons were killed and many more injured. Even the children and women were not spared. Horrified by the incident, Rabindranath Tagore, whom Gandhi called 'Gurudev' and who gave the epithet of 'Mahatma' to Gandhi, 'flung to the face of the Government his title of knighthood'. In 1920, Mahatma Gandhi participated in the Khilafat Movement.

Shocked by the events that took place after the passage of the Rowlatt Act and the Jallianwala Bagh massacre, Mahatma Gandhi, as he began to be addressed then, launched the Non-cooperation Movement. It envisaged renunciating government titles, boycotting government service, legislatures, schools, colleges and non-payment of taxes. The movement evoked a spontaneous response among the people in the country but it also resulted in violence at some places, particularly at Chauri Chaura in Uttar Pradesh where people set fire to a police station causing the death of twenty-two policemen. To avoid further bloodshed he withdrew the movement. For Gandhi, a believer in *satya* (truth) and *ahinsa* (non-violence) violence of any kind was the most abhorrent expression of human anger.

When the British Government realised that the Reforms of 1919 had not satisfied the Indian people, a Commission was appointed under the chairmanship of John Simon. Since it was an 'all white' Commission, it was boycotted on its arrival in India. Bapu, as Mahatma Gandhi was affectionately called, spearheaded the movement. The Congress Party adopted the Purna Swaraj Resolution (a resolution to achieve complete independence) in 1930 at its Lahore Session. On 6 April 1930, Bapu started the Civil Disobedience Movement with his historic march to Dandi to break the Salt Law imposed by the British-Indian Government. The movement, aiming at strikes, boycott of British goods and a general attitude of civil disobedience towards authority spread to all parts of the country.

On 5 March 1931, the Gandhi–Irwin Pact was signed and Gandhi agreed to end the Civil Disobedience Movement without any conditions. On 29 August 1931 Bapu sailed for London to attend the Second Round Table Conference which opened in London on 7 September 1931. He had earlier visited England four times and had walked the streets in the conventional dress of a pre-war English gentleman, in a well-cut morning coat and silk hat. Clad only in *dhoti* and a *chadar* the *Mahatma* or the 'half-naked seditious *fakir*' now became a legend, and fantastic stories—some kind and some unkind—spread about him. Winston Churchil's niece, Clare Sheridan, a sculptor, who sculptured Lenin's head in 1920, made studies of Bapu's head while Bapu sat spinning or meeting people at the Knightsbridge house where he spent the hours in-between the Conference at St James' Palace. She said: 'Gandhi, whom I place in the first rank of contemporary greatness, is also comparable with Lenin but in a different way, that is to say, spiritual rather than physical or intellectual ... To my mind, Gandhi's greatness is spiritual, and for this reason, he is greater, more formidable than any of the famous men of today. He has a spiritual awareness which humanity must develop if the world is ever to be raised out of the hell of its own making.' Bapu braved the harsh London winter clad only in his *dhoti* and a *chadar*. Some journalists asked him: 'Well, Mr Gandhi, Don't you think you are somewhat underclad?' 'Well,' Bapu quipped, 'the King has enough clothes on his person sufficient for both of us.' On his return to India, Gandhi once again started the Civil Disobedience Movement and was duly arrested.

Poets, saints and social reformers had, for centuries condemned untouchability in Hindu society but what Mahatma Gandhi did will always be remembered. When, in August 1932, the Communal Award was announced providing separate electorates for the 'untouchables', Bapu announced his intention to go on a fast unto death shocking millions of people into realising that they were guilty of promoting untouchability. After five days of suspense, leaders of upper-caste Hindus and of the so-called 'untouchables', whom Bapu had christened *Harijans* or children of God, signed a pact under which the proposal for separate electorates was given up for an increased share of reserved seats. The British Government accepted this formula as well and Bapu broke his fast.

Bapu settled down in a mud hut in a village near Wardha and devoted his thought and energy to the upliftment of *Harijans* and the development and propagation of the country's rural economy, and education. With the outbreak of war in 1939, Bapu was dragged back into the political maelstrom. He was not the man to sit back and shirk responsibility when danger threatened his people and a crisis seemed imminent. There were many within and outside the Congress who felt that this was the hour to strike, since Britain's difficulty was India's opportunity. But to Bapu such an attitude seemed immoral and inconsistent with the Congress creed. 'We do not seek our independence out of Britain's ruin,' he said.

In March 1940, the All India Muslim League, under the presidentship of M.A. Jinnah passed a resolution saying that Muslims were not a minority but a separate nation and the concept of Pakistan came into being. Bapu was distressed. His wife, Kasturba, who had supported him through his pursuits, passed away. Bapu was sad and heart-broken, yet his indomitable spirit did not sag. He continued his struggle, courting arrest and holding meetings at Sabarmati Ashram, near Ahmedabad. The Congress Party, at its meeting in Wardha in July 1942, passed a resolution asking the British Government to withdraw from India and threatened to launch a struggle. In August 1942, Gandhi launched the Quit-India Movement in an effort to bring the British to the negotiating table. Bapu was arrested along with other leaders precipitating a mass revolt. In 1945, the then British Viceroy, Lord Wavell, was called to London for consultations. The British Government tacitly accepted the two-nation theory, which culminated in the creation of India and Pakistan.

But unfortunately, even before the two-nation theory was accepted, riots broke out between Hindus and Muslims. These riots, engineered by fanatics belonging to both religions, deeply disturbed Bapu. When he found that these riots were becoming uncontrollable he undertook a fast unto death. As his condition deteriorated, wiser counsel prevailed among the people. The riots stopped and Bapu broke his fast. The country was partitioned into India and Pakistan on 15 August 1947.

On 30 January 1948, Nathu Ram Godse shot Bapu while he was moving towards a dais to attend his daily prayer meeting. Bapu uttered, 'Hey Ram', and collapsed dying with the Lord's name on his lips. For a deeply spiritual man, Bapu had little inclination towards religious fads and rituals. His visits to temples or centres of pilgrimage were rare. He never felt the urge to do so because to him service was the highest form of religion and for this a visit to the *Bhangi* (untouchable) colony was more appropriate than a tryst with a godman. He wrote in *My Experiments with Truth* of his first visit to Varanasi: 'Where one expected an atmosphere of meditation and communion, it was conspicuous by its absence. ... When I reached the temple, I was greeted at the entrance by a stinking mass of rotten flowers. The floor was paved with fine marble, which was however broken by some devotees innocent of aesthetic taste, who had set it with rupees serving as an excellent receptacle for dirt.'

When Bapu reached the *Jnanavapi* temple (Well of Knowledge) the surroundings had already spoiled his mood. He had no desire to make any *dakshina*, so he offered just a *pie* (small coin) to the *panda* (priest). The latter threw it away and swore at Bapu saying that the insult would take him to hell. Unperturbed, Bapu said: 'Maharaj, whatever fate has in store for me ... it does not behove one of your class to indulge in such language. You may take this *pie* if you like, or you will lose that, too.' The *panda* told him that he did not care for the *pie* and followed his remark with a volley of abuses. 'I took the *pie*,' writes Bapu, 'and went my way. But the Maharaj was hardly a man to let the *pie* go. He called me back and said, "Alright, leave the *pie* here, I would rather not be as you are. If I refuse your *pie* it will be bad for you".'

Mahatma Gandhi was appalled when he learnt in Calcutta, (now Kolkata), of animal sacrifice to appease Goddess Kali.

He writes: 'To my mind the life of a lamb is no less precious than that of a human being. I hold that the more helpless a creature, the more entitled it is to protection by man from cruelty of man.' His attitude towards cow protection, too, was more 'humanitarian' than religious. He did not worship the bovine species in the sense that some *gau-rakshaks* do today, but in a letter to Jawaharlal Nehru in 1925, he said: 'The cow is merely a type for all that lives. Cow protection means protection of the weak, the helpless, the dumb and the dead.' For Bapu this was the major reason to protect the poor animal. Once when he came home to see that Kasturba had lit a *ghee* lamp for *puja* to mark his birthday, he admonished her for wasting oil when millions in India had to eat their bread dry.

The Father of our Nation had very clear views on the role of the State in a secular polity. In 1946, he told a Christian missionary, 'I swear by my religion. I will die for it. But it is my personal affair. The State has nothing to do with it.' On 28 November 1947, speaking on Guru Nanak's birthday, he opposed the idea of the Somnath temple being constructed with State funds. 'A secular State cannot spend money on the basis of communities,' he said.

Even today, more that half a century after his death, the light that Bapu had shown us during his lifetime continues to guide people all over the world through times of violence and distrust. Like Buddha and Jesus Christ he provided us with what Dr Radhakrishnan called 'a moral axis'. He bequeathed to the world a philosophy that can be applied, adapted and assimilated to every situation. Bapu's message of non-violence, truth and justice, can be heard reverberating throughout the world, laying the foundation for a better future for mankind.

Veer Savarkar

$\mathcal{V}$eer Savarkar was a great nationalist and freedom fighter who, like Swami Dayananda and Sri Aurobindo, sought to reform Hindu society and place Hinduism in a national context. But Swami Dayananda and Sri Aurobindo were men of religion and in contrast Vinayak Damodar Savarkar had very little to do with matters of faith. He politicised religion and introduced religious metaphors into politics. He pioneered an extreme, uncompromising and rhetorical form of Hindu nationalism in Indian political discourse. His mission was to establish India as a Hindu nation and his unflinching faith in Hindu destiny made him sacrifice his life for the resurrection of Hindu glory.

Vinayak Damodar Savarkar was born on 28 May 1883 at Bhagur. The study of history and the epics interested him from his childhood. The atmosphere of bondage oppressed Savarkar even as a young boy. He was forever in search of an opportunity to liberate India from the fetters of British imperialism. He gathered around him his schoolmates, and in 1899, he formed a group called Mitra Mela, the 'beehive', as Sir Valentine Chitrol referred to it, of revolutionaries in western India. This organisation became Abhinav Bharat in 1904 and its network was spread over western and central India, England, France, Germany, America, Hong Kong, Japan, Singapore and Burma.

Savarkar's source of inspiration was Mazzini. It was Mazzini's *Young Italy* that in 1904 inspired Savarkar to name his secret organisation 'Abhinav Bharat.' Every member of this organisation took an oath to dedicate himself to fight for freedom. Savarkar's organisation rendered a new patriotic and political atmosphere and transformed the city into a political volcano. It dominated all the public and political institutions in Nasik, changed religious ceremonies and festivals into political and national functions. This atmosphere of heightened political activism gave the district authorities many sleepless nights.

Savarkar passed his Matriculation examination in December 1904 and left Nasik for Poona (now Pune) in January 1905, where he joined Fergusson College. Savarkar's striking personality and easy confidence won him many followers and soon a Savarkar group was formed which cast its spell on the entire college. The group started a hand-written weekly known as *Aryan Weekly* in which Savarkar often wrote illuminating articles on patriotism, literature, history and science. One of Savarkar's articles, *Saptapadi*, dealt with the seven stages of evolution. He also studied the dramas of Kalidasa and Bhavabhuti and was greatly influenced by Scott, Shakespeare and Milton. Very soon, he started giving lectures on the history of the world, the revolutions in Italy, the Netherlands and America.

In December 1905, Savarkar went to Bombay (now Mumbai) to study law. The activities of Abhinav Bharat continued simultaneously and it expanded to persons like B.G. Kher, J.B. Kripalani as its members. *Vihari*, a local

Marathi weekly, gradually became the mouthpiece of Abhinav Bharat. The organisation's leadership knew no caste distinctions; Savarkar himself shared food with non-Brahmin families. Savarkar believed that social and political revolutions were two wheels of the same chariot.

On 7 October 1905, Savarkar celebrated Vijaya Dashami in a novel manner. With a troop of firebrand students from Fergusson, the Abhinav Bharat leader collected cartloads of *videshi* (foreign) clothes and ceremoniously burned them at Pune's Lakdi Pul, thus imparting a modern nationalist connotation to the traditional Vedic fire sacrifice. Besides Savarkar, Tilak and S.M. Paranjpe also spoke at the first bonfire of foreign clothes in India. R.P. Paranjpe, the then principal, fined Savarkar ten rupees and expelled him from the college hostel. The action caused a wave of indignation including an editorial by Tilak. Savarkar was the first student from a government-aided educational institution in India to participate in the Swadeshi movement. To promote *swadeshi* (indigenous) articles, a *bazaar* (market) was opened in Tilak's own compound on 12 June 1906 where more than twenty thousand people visited sixty stalls. Similarly, a *swadeshi* fair was held in Bombay at Dadar where thirty stalls exhibited *swadeshi* articles. A big exhibition was organised at Pandharpur at the time of the Kartika fair on 25 September 1906.

Savarkar received a scholarship from Shyamaji Krishna Verma for the study of law and reached London in July 1906. London, in those days, was a veritable centre for revolutionaries from Russia, Egypt and even China. Here, he was admitted in Gray's Inn on 26 July for legal studies. But his prime motive was to study British politics and prepare himself to checkmate it. There, he proved to politically-minded Indian youth that peaceful revolution is more or less a misnomer when applied to the solution of such questions as the Indian political one. In London, he founded the 'Free India Society'. The society had regular meetings, celebrated Indian festivals, birth and death anniversaries of great Indian patriots, and discussed Indian political problems and their remedies and recruited more and more members.

In London, Savarkar was greatly influenced by the teachings of Mazzini. He translated his autobiography in Marathi and sent the manuscript to his brother. The book was printed in Pune in April 1907. The first edition of the book was sold out in three months. Later, his book, *1857: The First Indian War of Independence*, inspired many people into joining the struggle for freedom. This book was first written in Marathi and, on persistent demand, was translated into English. His pamphlet named *Khalsa*, and many others issued in Gurumukhi, motivated Sikh soldiers in enlisting their support for Indian independence. He wrote articles on Indian affairs in the *Gaelic America* of New York, got them translated into German, French, Italian, Russian and Portuguese languages and had them published in the respective countries with the sole aim to acquaint the civilised world with Indian affairs and make India a living issue in international affairs.

He even deputed Madame Cama and Sardar Singh Rana to represent India at the International Socialist Congress which was held on 22 August 1907 at Stuttgart in Germany. In spite of opposition from the British representative, Madame Cama, with the support of Hyndman of England and M. Jean Jaures of France, stood before the conference to move the resolution on India and unfurled a flag, symbolising Indian independence, designed by Savarkar. The resolution was intended to describe the continuance of British rule in India as most disastrous and extremely injurious to the interests of India. It urged the freedom-loving countries to cooperate in liberating India.

After completing his studies in London, Savarkar went to Paris where he stayed with Madame Cama. While he was in Paris, a bomb was thrown at Lord Minto and Savarkar's brother was implicated in the case. Savarkar returned to London, but as soon as he arrived at Victoria Station on 13 March 1910 he was arrested by a telegraphic warrant from the Government of Bombay under the Fugitive Offenders Act of 1881. He was charged with conspiracy to wage war against His Majesty the King Emperor of India. The Magistrate refused to release him on bail and he was sent to India for trial. When the steamer *S.S. Morea* was bringing him to India Savarkar escaped through a porthole and into the sea. He touched shore at Marseilles with a view to secure the protection of the French law. But the English guards caught him and brought him back to the ship.

Three trials, involving Veer Savarkar, were to be heard by the Special Tribunal. The first involved thirty-eight accused, including Veer Savarkar. The second involved him and Gopalrao Patankar. The third involved him alone. After sixty-eight days of protracted trial, he was sentenced to life imprisonment on 23 December 1910. Since the tribunal did not take cognisance of the legality of his arrest on French soil, the trial was indeed an outrage of international law. The Special Tribunal had passed judgement on a man whose case was sub judice in the International Court at the Hague. The same tribunal tried him in another case on 30 July 1911 and sentenced him to another term of life imprisonment. Savarkar was only twenty-seven at that time. Ordinarily, the very idea of the terrible sentence for half-a-century would have crushed even the stoutest heart, but Savarkar bore this colossal shock heroically. He asserted:

Don't be too hopeful of success. Be always prepared for the worst possible reverses. For those who are born in an age of despair and darkness must be prepared to face the grim struggle with the possibility of reverses, if they aspire for the dawn of a new era.

Savarkar was incarcerated in Dongri, Byculla, Thana and finally in the Andamans jails. He was given a very hard job in cellular jail. He was yoked to an oil-mill like a bullock, but he knew that each drop of oil that fell in the bucket would set the hearts of thousands of revolutionaries aflame. It was this thought that helped and inspired him in the dark, difficult, agonising solitary life in prison. He was made to eat foul food, live with rank criminals, denied human companionship and treated with utmost contempt.

In jail, Savarkar continued to read books on politics, literature, economics—the works of Spencer, Mill, Darwin, Huxley, Heckel, Emerson, Gibbon, Carlyle, Shakespeare, Milton, Dickens, Tolstoy, Kropotkin, Plato, Artistotle, Treitske, Nietzsche, Vivekananda and Ramatirth. He read all the Vedas, the Upanishads, the *Mahabharata* and the *Ramayana*. He also read Marathi poets from Jnyaneshwar to Moropant and studied the *Quran* and the *Bible*. He wrote poetry running into 13,500 lines by scratching on the prison walls. These poems were published under the title *Kamala* in the year 1922. His poetry contains Vedic, epic and historical ideas.

While Savarkar was in the Andamans, he found that once in a fortnight a Hindu convict would leave the Hindu rank during meal time and join the Muslim rank. He carried out a vigorous *shuddhi* movement for bringing forcibly converted Muslim convicts back to the Hindu fold. He also propagated the cause of Hindi. Within a few years, Hindi replaced Urdu in all matters affecting the Hindus. Later, he was taken to Ratnagiri and released conditionally on 16 July 1924 from the Yeravada jail. He was put in Ratnagiri and was released conditionally on 10 May 1937.

In 1930, the orthodox section of Brahmins decided to sabotage the growing campaign against untouchability. They passed a resolution barring untouchables from entering the temple during the Ganapati festival. Savarkar countered this move by organising a separate Ganapati festival for all Hindus. The idol was installed and worshipped by a Shiva *bhangi* (scavenger). The prize for reciting the *Gayatri Mantra* was also won by a *bhangi* boy. However, the crowning achievement of the anti-untouchability movement was in establishing the Patit Pavan Mandir for all Hindus.

Savarkar totally rejected the view that caste is determined by birth. In his view, the caste system should have been based on the virtues and work of individuals. The customs and traditions of castes were described by Savarkar as the seven chains that enslave Hindu society. He interpreted Indian history with a view to highlight the unparalleled achievements of Hindus in different areas of life. Hindus could march forward with confidence if they properly realised the achievements of their forefathers, he said.

Savarkar was a prolific writer. He wrote several essays on the politics of the time. His autobiography, *My Transportation for Life*, which depicts his jail life in the Andamans, is an inspiring work. Savarkar also wrote three plays: *Usshap, Sanyasta Khadga, The Foresaken Sword*, and *Uttarakriya*. As a dramatist, he did not care much for plot or stage effects. His primary focus was the characterisation, and Savarkar's characters moved with emotion and reason. *Moplah Rebellion* and *Transportation* are the two novels that he wrote.

Savarkar believed that there is a fundamental and natural difference between men and women. He did not like women to obey the dictates of old customs. He even regarded female education indispensable for the upliftment of a nation.

A woman should be a ministering angel rather than a masculine Amazon or a Virago, he said.

After 1937, the Hindu Mahasabha came under Savarkar's leadership. In his presidential address at the nineteenth session of the Akhil Bharatiya Hindu Mahasabha held at Karnavati, Ahmedabad, in 1937, Savarkar said,

> The Mahasabha is not in the main a Hindu Dharma Sabha but it is pre-eminently a Hindu Rashtra Sabha and is a Pan-Hindu organisation shaping the destiny of the Hindu nation in all its social, political and cultural aspects. It aims at the all-round regeneration of the Hindu people.

Savarkar was the main source of inspiration for the formation of the Indian National Army whose founder Rasbehari Bose, an Indian revolutionary settled in Japan, was fully committed to Sarvarkar's mission of militarisation and of armed revolution. Under Sarvarkar's leadership Hindus of all castes and creeds were successfully united for a political struggle. The announcement by British Prime Minister Attlee, that India would be divided into two nations deeply hurt Savarkar. His apprehension proved prophetic. The joy of independence was almost delirious but lasted hardly for forty-eight hours. Soon, the news of communal troubles began to cast deep gloom. The whole of the Punjab, east and west, had become a graveyard of destruction and death. The magnitude of the carnage stunned all. Nathu Ram Vinayak Godse shot Gandhi on 30 January 1948. In his early youth, Godse had been a worker of the Rashtriya Swayam Sewak Sangh (RSS). There was trouble and tension in a few cities between the Hindu Sabhaites and the RSS on one hand and the violent crowds of Gandhians on the other. The RSS was outlawed and the government accused Savarkar of complicity in the deed and put him behind bars. But later the court held him not guilty.

Savarkar pleaded that Hindutva was different from Hinduism. Hindutva embraces all the departments of thoughts and activity of the whole being of Hindu race. He said that every person who regards and owns this land of 'Bharatvarsha', as the land of the origin of his religion is a Hindu. In his endeavours to promote the concept of a Hindu nation, Savarkar's social objective remained encouraging a Hindu mind free from blind religiosity, spiritualism and unquestioning belief in the scriptures. He felt that change of religion meant change of nationhood. He asserted that conversion from Hinduism did not merely consist of the dismissal of idol-worship, polytheism, the revelation of the Vedas and the divinity of Rama and Krishna, but it brought in its wake the abandonment of emotional attitudes which was the very bulwark of this nation.

On 28 May 1958, on his seventy-fifth birthday, the Bombay Municipal Corporation held a public reception for Savarkar. On this occasion, he spoke of the need for strengthening the armed forces. He wanted to see India as mighty as the erstwhile Soviet Union. In 1965, his health began to deteriorate and on 26 February 1966 Vinayak Damodar Savarkar breathed his last.

Despite assertions to the contrary, Savarkar greatly admired Muslims. For him, they represented all that was deficient or missing in the Hindus. Though strongly committed to a Hindu God or *Dev*, and the idea of a Hindu *Rashtra*, he greatly admired the political and religious fervour of Islam. He said that while Muslims possessed qualities that made them unassailable, Hindus suffered limitations handed over to them by metaphysics and tradition. He wanted Hindus to learn a great deal from Muslims about building a commonly shared national life and consolidating the place of faith in their commonly shared lives. The Muslims were unified in their faith, which was lacking in the Hindus. This made them better equipped to take on their opponents. They had a sense of community that ultimately helped in bringing about a sense of national unity. On the other hand, Hindus were divided in terms of schools of philosophy, debilitating metaphysical propositions, castes and surfeit of conventions masquerading as traditions. Muslims acted under the direct command of God, had a notion of theocracy, which helped their militant campaigns against the *kafirs*. Hindus were left to reconcile doctrines, such as the *karma* theory and principled opposition to use of force, all of which lead to a disjuncture between theory and practice.

In short, the self had 'absorbed' a great deal of the non-self, leading it to redefine itself. The primary non-self in Savarkar's case was Islam and its followers. Savarkar had to ensure that the difference between the self and the non-self was not obliterated. The Hindu self had to maintain its identity and distinctiveness and at the same time be equal to the non-self in several important ways. This entailed a definition of the non-self by Savarkar. The tormentors had proved to be teachers. A great deal of what Savarkar had learned from Muslims would ultimately determine his conception of political Hindutva. He had to accept the brutal embrace of the intimate enemy. While the Hindu self had 'learned' and 'absorbed' several attributes of the non-self, it could not allow the non-self to emasculate its complete identity. The self had to remain distinct and have an autonomy of its own. Having begun on a premise that Hindus were deficient in several respects when compared to the Muslims, Savarkar now had the task of distancing himself from too close a comparison with the traditional adversary. After all, the Hindus and Muslims were, according to him, locked in a life and death battle for centuries. It was, therefore, important for Hindus to prove their strength and 'seek retribution for the wrongs done to them as a nation and as a race', he said. He felt that any attempt to extend a hand of friendship to the Muslims, or accept a hand extended by the Muslims, had to be based on perfect equality.

In 1927, Savarkar wrote a play called *Sangeet Uhshraap*. Untouchability among the Hindus, the decadence prevalent among upper-caste Hindus, untouchability leading to conversion to Islam, the limitations of Brahminical Hinduism and the Muslim agenda in India figures prominently as themes in the play. Desecration of Hindu temples, conversions by 'force or fraud', corrupting of Hindu girls and the overall destruction of Hinduism—these themes were to forever remain Savarkar's short-hand symbols for characterising Islam. Between 1921 and 1937, he wrote *Hindutva, Hindu-Pad-Padshahi*, *Uttarkriya*, and *Sanyastha Khadga*. In *Hindutva*, Savarkar quoted Ramdas, Shivaji's guru and mentor, who characterised Muslims as those who hated Hindusthan and had sinned against the Hindu God, and so were defilers of religion. His rhetoric against Muslims attained an all time high in the 1930s and early 1940s, especially as he increasingly reacted to the matching stridency and vitriol generated by Jinnah and the Muslim League. He questioned the fidelity of Muslims towards India and accused them of wanting to re-establish Muslim rule in India.

Savarkar's speeches, therefore, as President of the Hindu Mahasabha after 1937, are the clearest exposition of his vision of a Hindu *Rashtra*. There is a great deal of rhetoric in these public utterances in favour of an Indian State in which all citizens irrespective of caste and creed, race and religion are all treated alike on the principle of one man, one vote'. Consolidation and the independence of the Hindu Nation was, therefore, another name for the independence of the Indian Nation as a whole. He said that India's independence was inextricably linked to the independence of our people, our race, our nation, Hindus had to be masters of their own house and form the essence of political independence for India as well. The mastery of one's own house, for Savarkar, meant ensuring the primacy of the religion, race and cultural identity of the Hindus. Merely winning geographical independence, that is, independence of the Indian territory and the State, was not good enough, he said, and independent India must ensure and protect the Hindutva of the Hindus. He was emphatic that Hindutva was not a turban worn in a particular style, nor was it to be located in the pages of the *Brahmasutra*, or in the symbolism of a priest's tuft of hair, and least of all in cow-piss, *gomutra*. Hindutva, he wrote, is the life of a great race.

The gulf between Hindutva and Hinduism widened as Savarkar proceeded in his definition of Hindutva. According to him despite names like *Aryavrata*, Bharatvarsha or Bharatkhanda gaining currency, the world knew the inhabitants of this land as 'Hindus' and the land itself as 'Hindusthan'. What remained, therefore, was the conception of a national and cultural unity. From this he returned to the idea of territoriality and built another set of scaffolding around it. The most ancient name of our country, he maintained, was 'Sapta Sindhu' or 'Sindhu'. The river, Sindhu or Indus, after which the land and people derived their names, was the vital spinal cord that connected the remotest past to the remotest future. The land that lay between Sindhu, the river, and Sindhu, another name for the seas that surround peninsular India, was our whole Motherland, he said. It was a cohesive geographical unit, not merely a piece of land but a nation. What made it a nation was also the idea of cultural unity.

In this way, the first essential of Hindutva for Savarkar was a geographical one. 'Hindusthan', he wrote, 'was the land of the Hindus—and a Hindu was primarily a citizen either in himself or through his forefathers of "Hindusthan".' By implication, therefore, a Muslim resident of India would also be entitled to call himself a Hindu. But Savarkar rejected this claim. He qualified his stand saying, maybe, in some future day and age when all 'isms' cease to exist and when cultural and religious bigotry is a thing of the past, then the word 'Hindu' may come to indicate a citizen of Hindusthan and nothing else. The defining feature of Hindutva, according to Savarkar, was a commonly shared *sanskriti*, (culture). Hindus are one, said Savarkar, because they are a nation, a race and own a common *sanskriti*. The story of the civilisation of a nation, he said, is the story of its thoughts, its actions and its achievements. It was Sanskrit, he asserted, which formed the common link between all Indian languages. Common feasts and festivals and rites and rituals were the final arbiter of the essential unity of the Hindus. The different places of pilgrimage constituted the common inheritance of the Hindu race. The line of demarcation that divided Savarkar's categorisation of Hindutva and the term 'Hinduism' that he was so much at pains to distance himself from was very thin. A Muslim, argued Savarkar, could never be part of Hindutva because he did not own up and identify with the Hindu *sanskriti* as a whole. They belonged to a different cultural matrix. Their heroes, their objects of worship and their fairs and festivals had little in common with the Hindus. It was imperative for a Hindu to have 'uncommon and loving attachment to his racial *sanskriti*'. Muslims, in this way, were condemned to be a minority community. Savarkar lived in independent India for nineteen years during which time he advocated his brand of Hindutva and wrote and spoke extensively on the security and defense of India. The concept of Hindutva has been espoused by the Bharatiya Janata Party as an electoral weapon.

M.N. Roy

M.N. Roy was the founder of the political movement, known as Radical Humanism. As a philosophy of life, Radical Humanism covers the entire field of human existence from abstract thought to social and political reconstruction. It is the tradition of the revolt of man against the tyranny of God and his agents on this earth. Roy was a great revolutionary and a political activist, who had the unique opportunity of working with revolutionary figures like Lenin, Trotsky and Stalin. He participated in the armed struggle in India against the British Empire during the first two decades of twentieth century and also in the revolutionary activities in Mexico and China. It is rare that a political activist happens to be a scholar and a thinker, but Roy was both. His distinct and definitive approach differed from Mahatma Gandhi and Jawaharlal Nehru. He had better contacts both within and outside the country than any other leader in India. Even Nehru lacked the experience and vision that Roy possessed of the revolutionary movements in other lands.

The original name of Manavendranath or M.N. Roy was Narendranath Bhattacharya. He was known by this name during the first phase of his life, the phase of militant nationalism. Narendranath or Naren, as he was known in those days, was born in 1887 in Arbelia, a village not far from Calcutta (now Kolkata) in the district of 24 Parganas. His father, Dinabandhu Bhattacharya, was the head-priest of the temple of Goddess Ksheputeshwari in the village Ksheput in Midnapur district of south-west Bengal. Dinabandhu left the village and took a job as a Sanskrit teacher in the village of Arbelia. Narendranath was his fourth child, second by his second wife whom he married after the death of his first wife. The child was brought up and educated at Chingripota which also became the scene of his first action as a militant nationalist. He passed the entrance examination and enlisted himself as a student in the National College in Calcutta. In his early years, Narendranath absorbed a good deal of Sanskrit learning from his father, elder brother and others.

During the years when Narendranath was growing up, Bengal was passing through turbulent times which reached its peak during the days of the agitation against the partition of Bengal which took place in 1905. The idea of Motherland evoked by Bankimchandra Chatterji in his famous novel, *Anand Math*, and the song *Vande Mataram*, gripped the mind of Narendranath. Swami Vivekananda, who after his triumphant return from the United States, became the powerful spokesman of religious nationalism in the form of resurrected spiritual Hinduism, also influenced his sensitive mind. The young boy was already adventure-loving. He loved to walk long distances and wander about from orchard to orchard, for something distant, something beyond. He used to spend many nights in the cremation ground looking for ghosts. He was a restless soul. He visited the Ramakrishna Ashram at Belur and learnt from Sivnarain Swamy and collected information about revolutionaries and their activities.

Even at the age of fourteen, Narendranath was quite energetic and full of revolutionary enthusiasm. He acquainted himself with the problems in Bengal and joined the struggle for Indian independence. In 1905, he started attending anti-partition meetings held frequently in Calcutta along with his friends. As a result of their political activism they were debarred from taking the final examination. Later, the order was withdrawn and they were allowed to appear for the examination. Naren and his friends were avid readers of the *Bhagavad Gita*, Bankim Chatterji's *Anand Math*, Aurobindo Ghosh's *Bhavani Mandir* and other revolutionary literature of the period. But what impressed them most were the books of Swami Vivekananda.

Naren and his friends joined the Anushilan Samity, an organisation in Calcutta for physical, mental and moral regeneration of Bengali youth. It developed an underground wing, which became the centre of revolutionary activities all over Bengal. In the course of time, similar organisations were set up in many other towns, some as branches and others as independent centres. He came in close contact with Barin Ghosh who had already started the Bengali daily, *Jugantar*. Naren helped Ghosh to run the daily and is said to have written some articles for the newspaper. Later, he wrote a booklet in Bengali entitled *Mayer Dak* (Mother's Call) and when the police came to know of this, Naren was arrested. After joining the revolutionary movement he was initiated into the art of shooting and bomb-making. Bullets and bombs were the main instruments of the revolutionaries and were used to terrorise British officers and punish defectors from the ranks.

Naren committed the first political dacoity at Chingripota Railway Station on 6 December 1907 to secure funds for the revolutionary activities that had developed under the leadership of Jatin Mukherjee. He was arrested and a copy each of Barin Ghosh's *Bartaman Rananiti* (Strategy of Modern Warfare) and the manuscript titled *Mayer Dak* (Mother's Call) were seized from his possession. He was released on bail. In the course of a couple of years, Naren committed more political dacoities. He was arrested on bail and then he absconded. As a fugitive, he spent most of his time in Howrah and Sibpur. Under the leadership of Jatin Mukherjee, he organised a movement. He had political discussions with various groups and came up with ways and means to drive the British out of the country. He held socialistic views and never mixed religion with politics. He thought of a 'People's Government' as distinct from the government of the privileged few and felt convinced that the only way to establish such a government was revolution.

Naren was arrested in the Howrah–Sibpur Conspiracy Case and spent about nine months in jail in solitary confinement, the most excruciating experience for him. While in incarceration, Naren along with other revolutionaries drew up a plan of armed insurrection. After his release from the jail, Naren took up employment as an agent of the India Equitable Assurance Company. He also worked as a bill collector of a rice mill and a timber works. Later, he opened a restaurant which became a centre for the procurement of arms and exchange of information. It became popular amongst soldiers and sailors owing to the special dishes that Naren cooked for them. He undertook the task of uniting all the revolutionaries. Under the garb of a *sannyasi*, Naren visited places like Benaras, Allahabad, Agra and Mathura. In about a year, a united organisation was established with branches and contacts in Bengal and outside. It came to be known as the Jugantar Party.

Naren established contacts with Indian revolutionary groups in Europe, the United States, Burma, Indonesia and in places like Bangkok, Singapore, and Hong Kong. In the western hemisphere, there were strong revolutionary groups in Vancouver in Canada and in San Francisco in the United States. He went to Java, Germany and Indonesia in 1915 as 'C. Martin' in search of arms, ostensibly as agent of the Harry & Sons, Calcutta, but somehow or the other his mission failed. He was able to establish contact with Sun Yat-Sen and other leaders of the Chinese revolution. He went to China. He found himself in British custody for one night in the Chinese city of Tientsin. Towards the end of 1915, there was a revolt in the Chinese provinces of Yunan and Szechuan, bordering on Burma and India. The revolt was against Yuan Shi-kai's plan to restore monarchy. The rebels had plenty of arms. Sun Yat-Sen liked Naren's suggestion that the Chinese rebels should pass on some of their arms to Indian revolutionaries across the border and to get five million dollars from the German Ambassador for the purchase of those arms. If the money were available, Sun Yat-Sen would send his emissary to Yunan and then Naren was to proceed there to take over the 'precious cargo'. But the plan fell through because at the last moment the Germans were not ready to spend the large amount, which it required.

Naren arrived in the United States in June 1916. A newspaper reported that one Charles A. Martin had arrived and though he had declared that he was en route to Paris to study theology, he was believed to be a revolutionary. On learning this, Naren immediately changed his name to M.N. Roy and started his journey to the New World. In Stanford, Roy met many academicians and political workers. He made many friends. There, he married Evelyn Trent who became Roy's political collaborator and accompanied him to Mexico and Russia. She co-authored a couple of books with Roy and wrote from time to time for communist journals under the pen-name 'Shantidevi'. This continued till they separated in 1926. In New York, he began a systematic study of socialism. The transition to socialism was a big event in Roy's political career. He continued to work for the revolution. But the revolution that he visualised after his conversion to socialism was basically different from the revolution that he worked for as a militant nationalist. One visualised a new social order, while the other was restricted only to the overthrow of British rule.

Roy was arrested one day in Columbia University for violating the immigration laws of the United States. He was released on a personal security. He gave a slip to the police in New York and after a two-day train journey landed in Mexico in July 1917 without any money. There, he met two German officers whom he had met earlier in Indonesia. He was able to contact the President of the country and secure large funds which he used for developing the Socialist Party of Mexico and later for rendering asistance to Borodin and the Russian Trade Mission in Washington. He contributed articles to a leading daily newspaper, the *El Pueblo*. The articles were written in English and then translated into Spanish, the language of the country. A conference was held in Mexico City in December 1917 and the Socialist Party was launched. Roy was elected its General Secretary. His work was so impressive that nobody believed that Roy was a foreigner. He was required to draft the labour bill and accompany the Labour Minister to various places to pacify workers who were resorting to strikes. He also edited the party journal and played an important role in establishing the organisation. The activities of the Socialist Party strengthened and widened the social base of the government. Roy also met Michael Borodin, one of the leaders of the Bolshevik Party of Russia who completed Roy's conversion to communism.

Roy learned from him not only the intricacies of dialectical materialism but also the greatness of European civilisation and the appreciation of art and culture. With Roy's help, Borodin succeeded in securing a foothold in the New World for Bolsheviks. Roy presided over a conference which decided to change the name of the party to the Communist Party, the first in the world outside Russia. Thus, Borodin prepared the ground for Roy's visit to Moscow.

Roy left Mexico in November 1919 after spending more than two years there. A diplomatic passport was arranged for him. Mexico's representatives in European countries were advised to render him any assistance that he might need. He reached Moscow in April 1920, anxious to work for the revolution in India by learning from the revolution located in Moscow. He was introduced to the leaders of the Comintern, including Lenin, Zinoviev, Trotsky, and Stalin. Lenin complimented Roy on his work in Mexico and stated that it could show the way to communist work all over the world. Roy attended the second congress of the Comintern as the representative of the Communist Party of Mexico, but for practical purposes, he was treated as the representative of India. He was elected to various bodies and was assigned the task of carrying the revolution to the East and more particularly to India.

Roy left for Tashkent with two train-loads of a variety of arms and a large treasure. The idea was to establish a base in Afghanistan and use the arms and the treasure to win over frontier tribes and through them establish contacts with revolutionary elements in India. But the plan had to be dropped owing to lack of cooperation from the Government of Afghanistan. The arms and the military officers who accompanied them proved useful eventually for subduing the British inspired revolts and for imparting military training to Indian *Muhajirs*.

Roy studied the *Quran* and other religious books of Islam. While taking care not to hurt the religious sentiments of the people he began to justify the revolution on the ground of equality preached by Islam. That removed the misgivings of the people. The Emir and the Khan were eventually subdued through military operations and revolution was spread to Bokhara and Khiva. By that time, about thirty to forty thousand Indians who were bent upon going to Turkey to fight for the Khilafat had entered the area. Some of them were captured by Turkoman rebels and were grossly ill-treated. Roy sent a detachment of the Red Army for their rescue. After rescue, they were taken to Bokhara where Roy had talks with them. They were provided with military training. In October 1920, the Communist Party was also formed in Tashkent. Roy went to Moscow where he wrote an important book, *India in Transition*. It provides the first ever analysis of the Indian situation from the Marxist point of view. The book was also translated into Russian, German and many other languages. The book was sold well in Europe and the USA.

While abroad Roy kept himself well-informed of the happenings in India during the year. He never regarded the Congress Party as the political party of the bourgeoisie. To him, it was a mass movement of immense potentiality, but saddled with a reactionary leadership. Roy wanted the leadership to be thrown out and replaced by a revolutionary leadership. In 1927, the Comintern sent Roy to China as its representative to supervise the implementation of a new thesis that it had adopted. He played a major role in drafting the thesis that was adopted by ECCI at its meeting in Moscow in November 1926.

When Roy returned to India he was a full-fledged communist. He had distanced himself from the Comintern but not with communism. The old leaders of the party were in jail, involved in the Meerut Communist Conspiracy Case. The leadership was in the hands of a young inexperienced group. After his return to India, and for many years thereafter, the worst hostility that Roy had to face was from the CPI, the Comintern and its adherents. The CPI was not happy with Roy's return to India. When Roy returned, the Civil Disobedience Movement was already on the decline. He and his supporters tried to stop the decline through agitation and propaganda amongst Congressmen but in the end, the movement was withdrawn on the basis of the Gandhi–Irwin pact.

As a result of his revolutionary activities, Roy was arrested in Bombay (now Mumbai) on 21 July 1931 and was taken to Kanpur to stand trial for his part in the Kanpur Communist Conspiracy. He was sentenced to twelve years' imprisonment, which on appeal, was reduced to six years. While in jail, he maintained contact with the outside world. He wrote a number of letters, articles, manifestoes and a book, *China in Revolt*, published under the pen-name of S.K. Vidyarthi in 1935. *My Experiences in China* and *Our Task in India* followed it. He was not allowed to make the defence statement, which was later published as *My Defence*. Some of his letters were published as *Letters to the Congress Socialist Party* and some of his articles were published in *The Mahratta* of Pune and *The Advocate* of Bombay. But his identity was never established. Ordinarily, Roy was a well-behaved prisoner. Officially, he wrote only one letter a month to Ellen Gottschalk, who, after Roy's release, came to India, married him and made India her home. Roy found in Ellen Roy not only a loving wife but also an intelligent helper and close collaborator. The letters were published in 1941 as *Letters from Jail*. They provide a glimpse of Roy's wide knowledge and all-embracing interests. Life in jail shattered Roy's health. In 1934, he became so alarmingly ill that during summer months he was removed to Almora and brought back again to Bareilly after the summer was over. The next year, he was taken to Dehra Dun when the weather became hot and kept there until his release.

Roy suffered from dilation of heart and pain in the chest and slow fever from time to time. Many eminent persons, including Albert Einstein, made representations to the Governments of India and England to show him humane treatment. Jawaharlal Nehru also took personal interest in the matter, but to no avail. As an undertrial he was an A class prisoner but after conviction he became a B class prisoner. But in spite of his ill-health Roy did plenty of writing in jail. He wrote about one thousand pages, which are strictly legal in nature. He was released from the Dehra Dun jail on 20 November 1936, after a jail term which lasted five years and four months. The Congress leaders received him. In his first statement to the people he asked the countrymen to rally in millions under the flag of the National Congress as a determined army fighting for democratic freedom. He expressed his desire to formally enrol himself as a member of the Congress. On release, he brought with him the manuscript of a thousand pages prepared in the prison. It was published as several books: *Fascism, Materialism, Historical Role of Islam, Ideals of Indian Womanhood.* A part of the manuscript remained unpublished, but was later published as *M.N. Roy's Memoir* by Allied Publishers.

Roy attended the Faizpur session of the Congress held in December 1936. Jawaharlal Nehru welcomed Roy into the Congress fold as a veteran freedom fighter. In his speech, Roy outlined a concrete programme of action to involve the people in the national struggle by identifying it with the struggles for their immediate demands. The speech had a profound effect upon the audience. In April 1937, he began the publication of his weekly journal, *Independent India,* to express his views on national and international developments. The Roy Group became more active after Roy's release. Its membership increased and it became a powerful factor in the political and the trade union field. Later, in the year, he toured Tamil Nadu and Andhra Pradesh. He went to Bengal, the land of his birth, where he was welcomed as a hero and was heard with rapt attention. He and his wife now settled down in Dehra Dun.

In 1940, Roy was elected President of the Congress. He delivered many lectures on Marxism and Communism and social revolution. He was the only leader to stress the necessity for a philosophical revolution. In September 1939, the Second World War started. The Congress began by resigning ministerial offices as a protest against the Viceroy's action involving India in the war without consulting the Central Legislative Assembly or the leaders of the people. It then moved on to the position of conditional cooperation. But the Viceroy and the British Government refused to fulfil the conditions and thus pushed the Congress in the direction of a struggle which culminated in the Quit India Movement in August 1942. Roy approved neither the course the Congress had adopted nor its attitude towards the war. He tried to persuade the Congress leaders not to adopt a hostile attitude towards the war. He prepared a thesis on the war which explained how it was not an imperialist but an internecine war which did not invite the application of the Leninist dictum of opposition to an imperialist war. The catastrophic developments in Europe had a profound effect on him. Roy resigned from the Congress when his suggestion that demonstrations, expressing sympathy and solidarity with France, which had just been conquered by Hitler, be organised all over the country was refused.

After discovering the faults and shortcomings of communism, in the last phase of his life, Roy moved away from communism and began his journey towards radical humanism. After the War, he re-examined many communist doctrines and theories. He was shocked and distressed when he found Stalin throwing away the moral leadership of progressive forces which was his, and trying to embark on a military conquest of Europe at the end of the war. He found in communism an utter disregard of and contempt for man, who had been reduced to the position of a helpless pawn in the hands of blind economic forces and an insignificant unit in the broad collectivity of a class. That happened under capitalism also. Neither capitalism nor communism showed the way out of the crisis. He thought of organised democracy and cooperative economy as a solution to the crisis which had gripped the world and was dragging it in the direction of war and destruction. He thought that both the organised democracy and cooperative economy should have a philosophical foundation. Freedom is the basic value in radical humanism. As a philosophy of life, it covers the entire field of human existence from abstract thought to social and political reconstruction. It does not believe in transcendentalism. Roy explained that radical humanism had taken over the tradition of the founders of modern civilisation, the tradition of the revolt of man against the tyranny of God and his agents on this earth.

Roy was anxious to retire from politics, settle down in Dehra Dun and devote himself completely to reading and writing. In 1946, the RDP decided to contest elections to the provincial assemblies. Roy had to play a major role in guiding and organising the election campaign. He was anxious that transfer of power should be made to the people and not to political parties claiming to represent them. But he did not succeed in his mission. He wrote extensively on national and international affairs in his own journal, re-named *Radical*

Humanist, in English and American journals. He now thought that revolution was a necessity but it was not possible to bring it about through the old method of armed insurrection owing to the tremendous military power of modern states. The new way, he thought, was through persuasion. His contributions to the discussions at Dehra Dun Camp are collected together in a book *New Orientation* published by the Renaissance Publishers of Calcutta. Radical Humanism brought Roy nearer to Mahatma Gandhi and his school of thought. Roy's own ideas about Mahatma Gandhi also underwent a big change in the last couple of years of the latter life. Roy realised that Mahatma Gandhi was a big moral force. He was shocked when he received news of Mahatma Gandhi's assassination.

Roy wrote more books, the most prominent of which is *Reason, Romanticism and Revolution*. Its first volume was published in 1953 and the second a year later after his death. It provides the quintessence of Roy's theoretical basis for the philosophy of radical humanism. Roy now needed rest and went to Mussoorie in June 1952 with his wife. While returning from his morning walk along a hill track there he stumbled, fell and rolled down the hill about fifty feet below. He sustained grave injuries and had to stay in bed for several weeks. When he recovered, he returned to Dehra Dun and began thinking of resuming his work. By May 1953, he started planning a visit to the United States for medical treatment and for fulfilling many engagements. But in August he had an attack of cerebral thrombosis. His condition deteriorated, and on 25 January 1954, he expired. Thus ended his untiring life which had been full of trials and tribulations and sustained struggle to uphold his beliefs and ideals in the face of strong opposition.

Ganesh Shankar Vidyarthi

Ganesh Shankar Vidyarthi, a great martyr, the embodiment of national unity, national integration, communal amity and universal brotherhood, was the founder of Sewa Dal, Sewa Ashram at Narwal in Kanpur, and Hindustani Biradari. Starting as a Home Rule Leaguer in pre-independent India he outshone his other contemporary leaders as a Swarajist and Congressman. As a social activist, a revolutionary, a national leader, as a journalist, as a legislator, and as a preceptor of non-violence he made enviable contributions in the Indian Trade Union movement, to the cause of farmers and endeared himself to the masses.

Martyrs are born and not made. This was as true of Ganesh Shankar Vidyarthi as of others. Born on 26 October 1890, in the Attarsuiya *mohalla* of Allahabad city, in a reasonably well-off family, Ganesh was the son of Gomti Devi and Babu Jai Narain. His father was an assistant teacher in Hindi in the Anglo-Vernacular School of the erstwhile Gwalior State. His mother was a woman of sterling character. The fearlessness inherent in Ganesh was the gift from his mother. She was religious-minded and god-fearing. Although not educated, she was highly learned and cultured and was very fond of relating to children stories with moral themes.

When Ganesh was born, his mother was living with her mother in Mungaoli. Ganesh and his mother could stay at Mungaoli only for a short period. In October 1892, they went to Saharanpur, where Ganesh's grandfather, on mother's side, Suraj Prasad, was posted as assistant jailor in the District Jail. At that time, bread was manufactured in jails and Ganesh's grandfather purchased that bread almost everyday and gave it to him. The child incidentally became very fond of the jail bread, knowing little that one day he would have to subsist on that very bread in jails. In Mungaoli, Ganesh was taught Urdu. In 1901, when his father was transferred to Bhilsa, Ganesh had an opportunity to read *Bangbasi* and *Bharat Mitra*, Hindi newspapers of Calcutta (now, Kolkata). By 1995, he had passed English Middle examination with Hindi as the second language. He was sent to Kanpur to get some job with the help of his elder brother. There, his uncle purchased for him books prescribed for the Entrance Examination of the University of Allahabad to enable him to prepare for the examination as a private candidate. Arrangement was made for his coaching in English and Mathematics and he passed the examination in 1907 in Second Division. He was admitted to the eleventh class in the Kayastha Pathshala College, Allahabad.

By that time, Allahabad had become a hub of political and literary activities and leaders like Bal Gangadhar Tilak, Bipin Chandra Pal and Gopal Krishna Gokhale visited the city to muster support for the Indian National Congress. Hindi Periodicals like *Pradeep, Swarajya, Karmayogi* and *Abhyudaya* carried articles on freedom of press, slavery, revolutionary upsurge and even cult of the bomb. Ganesh, as a student, was attracted towards political journalism and started working in the *Swarajya's* office. Its editor was convicted and sentenced to three and a half years of incarceration and the weekly was warned. Its four other editors were sentenced each to ten years of transportation for preaching sedition and were sent to Andaman and Nicobar islands, yet Ganesh escaped their fate due to ill-health and returned to Kanpur in February 1908. Excessive reading and writing affected his eyes adversely and he was advised to discontinue his studies only after eight months. He could not complete his education in Allahabad.

But Ganesh Shankar was able to interact with the leading literary figures of his time. At Kanpur, he started writing for the *Karmayogi*, a fortnightly review in Hindi. It reproduced translations of important extracts from Aurobindo Ghose's *Karamyogni* and Bal Gangadhar Tilak's *Kesari*. It published independent articles on principles of nationalism, *swadeshi* and boycott movements, national education and *Swaraj*. Revolutionaries frequented the place where he lived with his brother and Ganesh developed intimacy with them. The *Karmayogi* ceased its publication by 1910 at the instance of the government and *Swarajya* too had to be stopped as eight of its editors were prosecuted. Ganesh had to join the local Currency Office in Kanpur on a paltry sum of thirty rupees per month from 6 February 1908. But after seven months he had to resign when his officer objected to his reading a book while in the office.

On 1 December 1908, Ganesh Shankar joined Pandit Prithvinath High School in Kanpur as a teacher. But after a year he was forced to resign the post again due to his habit of reading *Karamayogi*, which was regarded as a seditious paper. In Kanpur, he became a member of the Hindu Friends Association and came in contact with the elite of the town who introduced him to Acharya Mahavir Prasad Dwivedi who became his Guru in journalism. He served as a private secretary to Seth Ram Gopal for some time, and later worked with Hindustan Insurance Company at Kanpur. But whatever money he received he spent on the purchase of books on Homoeopathy and Electrotherapy, and boxes of medicine. He began distributing medicines to members of his family and to his neighbours. He experimented and discovered that smaller doses of lower potency were quite useful.

At the age of nineteen Ganesh Shankar was married to Prakash Devi. The bride was sixteen years of age at that time. This matrimonial alliance between the two was cordial and happy. While Ganesh Shankar remained engrossed in the editorial and presswork, Prakash Devi managed the household and looked after the family. Even when he entered politics and courted arrest she rose to the occasion and became a tower of strength to him and supported his decision to court arrest.

Ganesh Shankar's contact with the editor of the monthly magazine *Saraswati*, Acharya Mahavir Prasad Dwivedi, brought him the post of assistant editor of the monthly in November 1911. His dedication and knowledge of the work endeared him to the editor. Dwivedi and Ganesh Shankar remained very close to each other. While working with the *Saraswati*, he translated a number of English stories into Hindi which were published under the title *Shekhchilli ki Kahaniyan*. It was his first book in Hindi. He was able to develop his creative faculty of writing in Hindi. He also developed his own literary style. His writings in the *Abhyudaya* attracted attention of the masses..

During 1907 to 1913, Ganesh Shankar faced some pecuniary difficulties and physical ailments. His studies abruptly ended. At times, he was unemployed. He came in contact with revolutionaries. For him, service to the nation and country was uppermost. While he was a student, he was quite impressed with Charlotte M Young's book, *Book of*

Golden Deeds. He felt inspired to start writing a book, *Our Renunciation for the Benefit of Others*. It contained stories of Indian heroes who had made sacrifices for others and had become great.

Ganesh Shankar joined *Abhyudaya* on 29 December 1912 as he was interested in a literary journal. He continued there till September 1913. The journal was running at a loss and with the joining of Ganesh Shankar, its circulation increased considerably. He used to write articles and even editorials for the paper. Simultaneously, he read the works of George Bernard Shaw, Upton Sinclair, Shelley, Stuart Mill, Tolstoy, Spencer, Rousseau, Maupassant, Ruskin, Carlyle, Thoreo, Shakespeare, Tennyson, Browning, H.G. Wells, and others. He was fascinated with the work of Victor Hugo and translated his masterpiece, *Les Miserables*, under the title *Ahuti*. In 1921, he also translated his work, *Ninetythree*, and an article captioned 'Glimpses of Political Revolution.' He also wrote on Joan of Arc, Maxim Gorky and Peter Kropotkin, the great anarchists. He read the political writings of the great political leaders of India. By this time, he had not only become a famous Hindi writer, but had also delved into the works of Surdas, Tulsidas, Kabirdas, Bhartendu Babu Harishchandra and Acharya Mahavir Prasad Dwivedi. He now earned the appellation of 'Vidyarthi', a lifelong student, and started writing his name as Ganesh Shankar Vidyarthi.

In 1913, Ganesh Shankar Vidyarthi started a weekly, *Pratap*, at Kanpur. In two of its forceful editorials in November 1913 it highlighted the plight of the oppressed Indians in South Africa. It outrightly condemned the practice of *Teen Kathia* in indigo plantation farms, called upon the people to oppose such a tyranny and bemoaned the inactivity and imbecility of the Government of Bihar. It openly opposed the repression of workers in indigo plantations by Europeans.

Due to the publication of the sensational and inflammatory pamphlet entitled '*Cawnpur ki Khuni Dastan*' the Government took action against it and the Comrade. In UP, from 1914 to 1918, the newspapers came under active surveillance. Having worked with the *Swarajya*, the *Karmayogi* and the *Abhyudaya*, Ganesh Shankar Vidyarthi was well aware of the tentacles of the Press Act. He fearlessly continued his advocacy of the peasants working in Champaran indigo plantations, the coolie emigrants in overseas colonies and the mill workers at Kanpur. He was warned thrice by the Government for spreading hatred against the European subjects of His Majesty. As the leading Hindi weekly, the *Pratap* had been publishing patriotic poems. Some of the poems were declared seditious and the security of the newspaper was forfeited.

The *Pratap* ceased publication for some time. But the paper had public sympathy. The money required was soon collected and deposited. The newspaper resumed publication. The newspaper reached its unexpected circulation. A Trust was created and the newspaper was registered. It continued to champion the cause of the *kisans* and workers. In 1921, it highlighted the agrarian disturbances in the districts of Rae Bareilly and Sultanpur. It published the reports of the riots in its issues, and compared repression to Dyer's massacre at Jallianwala Bagh, Amritsar. The then Governor Harcourt Butler felt unnerved. The Government initiated action against the Editor. When Vidyarthi found that the assets of the Pratap Press were in jeopardy he submitted his resignation. He was arrested and was incarcerated on 23 October 1921. He was released on 23 May 1922. He recorded his reminiscences of jail life in a diary and subsequently wrote *Glimpses of Jail Life* in twelve serials, published in the *Pratap*. From 22 November 1920, the *Pratap* weekly announced the publication of daily *Pratap* as well. Within a few days, the number of subscribers of the daily *Pratap* rose to five thousand. Due to adverse circumstances, it was closed down on 6 July 1921.

Ganesh Shankar Vidyarthi, in his ardent zeal to champion the cause of the poor *kisans* and to expose the corrupt and tyrannical officers, was involved in contempt cases. In 1926, the editor and the printer of the *Pratap* were again hauled up in the Mainpuri Court for contempt. The *Pratap*, in its defence, filed as many as thirteen specific cases of bribe taking. The editor was once charged with having committed a libel by publishing a distorted version of *baredada* (elderly) Maharaj Dhuniwale, in its issue of 25 September 1927. In the article, evil practices and vulgar rituals performed were exposed. The *Pratap* was also involved in another contempt case in the High Court of Allahabad. It published reports about the riot in Naini Jail on 22 April 1928 and a note entitled '*Dublish*' (an accused in the Kakori Train Dacoity Case). The High Court of Allahabad treated that as contempt of the honourable court and issued notice against the *Pratap* for contempt of court. But in spite of all this, Ganesh Shankar Vidyarthi never compromised the honour of his own and the country.

Politics was ingrained in Ganesh Shankar Vidyarthi's blood. As an editor of the *Pratap*, he had been publishing editorials highlighting the importance of self-rule propagated by Annie Besant. It asserted, when thousands of Indians overseas were subjected to the tyranny of colonial rule in Fiji, Jamaica, South Africa and other colonies, and wrote that Indians should not be afraid of raising a voice for Home Rule or *Swarajya*. As member of Home Rule League branch at Kanpur, he toed an independent line about controversies between Annie Besant and Mahatma Gandhi. He became

Mahatma Gandhi's follower. The *Pratap* published editorials on the role of Mahatma Gandhi and the Champaran Enquiry Committee as well as the European Associations.

Ganesh Shankar Vidyarthi served the cause of downtrodden, the exploited and poverty-stricken labourers, mill workers and the peasants. He worked hard to study the problems facing the *kisans* in UP and developed a liking for the rural atmosphere. To satisfy his urge for rural atmosphere he started visiting Narwal village, forty km from Kanpur and ten km from Sarsaul, the nearest railway station. He started delivering inspiring speeches there and exhorted the downtrodden peasants to stand up and unite against the landlords. He became quite popular in the countryside. During 1919 and 1920, he was elected as a delegate to the Nagpur Congress. When non-cooperation movement was launched, Vidyarthi became an ardent *satyagrahi*. With his efforts Narwal became a live centre for social, cultural and political activities. Vidyarthi was elected Secretary of the Kanpur Congress Reception Committee.

After the plenary session of the Congress at Kanpur in 1925, Ganesh Shankar Vidyarthi established an *ashram* on the model of Bardoli at Narwal. He became its President. In 1930, the *ashram* provided an excellent training ground for salt *satyagrahis*. The villagers were taught to prepare salt themselves and thus break the salt laws. The *ashram* provided as many as 400 volunteers who courted arrest, and thus defied salt laws. A number of reading rooms and spinning centres were opened in the adjoining villages. The *ashram* got accretion of land when some landlords donated their garden. With a view to check the widening schism between the two communities, he took the opportunity to convene a meeting of leading Hindus and Muslims in *Pratap*'s office to discuss the formation of an organisation which could foment common brotherhood. Its motto was that every citizen of India was first a Hindustani and religion was secondary to Indianhood. With this aim in view, an All-India Hindustani Biradari was established. He was elected its founder-president. He even favoured inter-communal marriages, but the time was not opportune for that. The Biradri propagated inter-community mess and conferences.

In November 1926, Ganesh Shankar Vidyarthi won the UP Council's elections by an overwhelming majority. The Swarajist Party in the UP Legislative Council consisted of twenty-three members and Ganesh Shankar Vidyarthi was one of them. Pandit Govind Ballabh Panth acted as its leader. Ganesh was a forceful legislator and his performance in the Council from 1927 to 1929 ranked him among the great parliamentarians of pre-independence India. His contribution in the form of debates, speeches and searching questions, national as well as local, was remarkable. He chose Hindi as the medium. He was always well prepared and worked hard to collect facts. In the Council, he championed the cause of farmers, the Trade Union and the mill-workers. He enjoyed the confidence of the Mazdoor Sabha and was elected Chairman. In 1928, when the Jail Inquiry Committee in UP started its work, he took an active part in this. The plight of prisoners in jail attracted his attention. He met the prisoners in the Central and Borstal jails and talked to Bhagat Singh and Batukeshwar Dutt at length. The Government had not only deprived them of their freedom, but had also kept them along with thieves, rogues and robbers. No books were allowed to them. They were given dirty and unpalatable food. Ganesh Shankar Vidyarthi condemned the attempt to artificially feed the prisoners who went on a hunger strike.

During 1927, Hindu-Muslim riots took place in Lahore, Bihar, Punjab, CP and UP. The Congress Committee organised a conference in October to evolve a formula for Hindu–Muslim unity. It empowered the AICC to appoint a Committee in each province for propaganda work in this connection. The Conference succeeded in evolving a formula, which was adopted with suitable modifications. Several important resolutions, including the one on Punjab communal murders, were adopted. Ganesh Shankar Vidyarthi lent full support to unity efforts within the Congress as well as within the community. He wrote a stirring editorial in the *Pratap* on the Calcutta Unity conference.

Ganesh Shankar Vidyarthi was a great freedom fighter. Through the columns of the *Pratap* in its issue dated 3 January 1930 he announced the Independence Day on 26 January. He proclaimed the ideal of *Purna Swarajya* by taking independence day pledge from all. Flag hoisting was done at 8 am, and processions were taken out thereafter. A solemn pledge to carry out the Congress instructions, issued from time to time, for the purpose of establishing *Purna Swarajya*, was taken. At Kanpur, the day was celebrated with unprecedented enthusiasm. The Congress Working Committee, at its meeting held at Sabarmati on 14 February 1930, resolved that civil disobedience was to be initiated and controlled by those who believed in non-violence for the purpose of achieving *Purna Swarajya*, as an article of faith. The UP Pradesh Congress Committee, at its meeting held on 26 February 1930, under the presidentship of Ganesh Shankar Vidyarthi also decided to recommend to the Congress Working Committee that Mahatma Gandhi be authorised to start civil disobedience movement and UPPCC would lend him utmost support and cooperation. A conference was held at Kanpur in April 1930. Preparations were going on for launching *satyagraha*. Ganesh Shankar Vidyarthi addressed an audience of fifteen thousand on 5 April. Agitation was intensified.

Having piloted the *satyagraha* successfully throughout UP, Ganesh Shankar Vidyarthi was arrested on 25 May 1930 and was sentenced to one year's rigorous imprisonment. Vidyarthi chose not to appeal when asked by his friends. While he was in Hardoi jail, the finances of his family worsened. His sons and daughters were studying. He had four daughters and the eldest was of marriageable age. His wife was mostly on sick bed. But all this did not deter him. Vidyarthi was released on 10 March 1931. On the execution of Bhagat Singh, Sukhdev and Shivram Rajguru at Lahore on 23 March 1931 Vidyarti gave a call for *hartal* (strike) at Kanpur on 24 March. There was a large-scale violence. He reached there and started rescuing victims from the houses that had been set on fire. The rescued persons included both Hindus and Muslims. He was alone in the riot-stricken area. The place was near a mosque. He was asked to address a gathering of about two hundred persons. In the act of saving the trapped persons he himself became the riot victim. Some people started attacking him with *lathis*. As the assassin approached him he bowed his head down only to be mowed down. He was then stabbed in the back and another man attacked him with a *khanta* (an axe). He fell down and after two days his body was found lying stuffed in a gunny bag in a hospital. He was cremated on 29 March 1931.

Thus ended this magnificent life for the cause of national unity at the age of only forty-one years. Due to the prevailing communal tension in the city, most of his admirers could not pay him their last homage. Jawaharlal Nehru described this great martyr as the 'true brave Congressman' and *The Tribune* praised Ganesh Shankar Vidyarthi's selfless devotion and for his fearless manner in which he met his death. With his freedom from communal bias he endeared himself to all parties and communities. He died for the noble cause and joined the ranks of the martyrs, thus becoming an example of supreme courage and devotion to duty. His was a rare example of heroism acclaimed by all Indians and Europeans alike.

Subhas Chandra Bose

*I*n the nineteenth century when India was still oppressed by British rule, two movements which tried to emancipate India from one of the darkest periods of her history were born—the Brahmo Samaj in 1828 and the Arya Samaj in 1876. The Brahmo Samaj attuned the minds of many Indian leaders to new ideas of democracy and freedom while the Arya Samaj aimed at reviving Indian culture among orthodox Hindus led to militant Hinduism. For the first time, it gave real unity to Hindu India, built up a combative nationalism and infused in the Indian people a sense of pride in their glorious heritage and extreme self-confidence which resulted in political extremism.

Subhas Chandra Bose was a great revolutionary who fought valiantly for India's independence. He was greatly influenced both by Vivekananda and Bankim Chandra. Vivekananda's philosophy and speeches on practical Vedanta and Indian spirituality created a deep impression on the minds of Indians. Bankim Chandra, on the other hand, exercised great influence upon the nationalistic spirit of Indians and channelled religious discussion towards a political direction. This fusion of religion and politics excited many young Hindu Bengalis. Bankim Chandra gave a concrete image of the motherland in his epoch-making novel *Ananda Math*. The immortal song, *Bande Mataram*, had a pivotal place in it. Bankim Chandra identified the individual with the country and expected maximum sacrifice from him in the cause of the motherland. By identifying the motherland with Durga, Lakshmi, Kali and Saraswati, he laid the foundation of spiritual nationalism and made patriotism into a religion.

Subhas Chandra Bose was born on 23 January 1897 at Cuttack, in Orissa. He was the sixth son and the ninth child of Janakinath and Prabhavati Bose. Janakinath was a Government Pleader and Public Prosecutor. He was a deeply religious, kind-hearted man and had a soft-corner for the poor and the needy. He took active interest in the social and educational institutions in Cuttack and was very liberal in distributing charities to poor students. He was a regular visitor at the annual sessions of the Indian National Congress, though he never took an active part in politics. The large Bose family gave little chance to Subhas to really thrive and develop. This affected him psychologically at an early age and he became an introvert. His father, with his strict reserved behaviour, overawed him. His mother dominated the domestic scene and, as far as family affairs were concerned, hers was usually the last word. As a child, Subhas yearned for a more intimate relationship with his parents and envied those children who had friendly relations with their parents. The presence of a large number of brothers and sisters in the family added to his feelings of utter insignificance.

At the age of five, Subhas was sent to an English elementary school in Cuttack from where he finished the seven years' course with top honours. In those days, only children of rich parents could have access to education which was, of course, costly. Subhas felt frustrated by the racial discrimination practised in his English school. In such schools, Indian students were not admitted to the Sports Club, or the Volunteer Corps and they could not take scholarship examinations either. This discrimination made Subhas conscious of the two different worlds existing in India—one representing the arrogant attitude of racial superiority in a school run on European lines and the other representing his family and the Indian society. He was extremely hurt by the discrimination practised in his school and developed a sense of isolation. However, yoga helped him develop a sense of confidence. When Subhas came in contact with Ramakrishna Paramahansa and Vivekananda, he began to believe that spiritual realisation could be attained through service of humanity. He decided to gain first-hand knowledge about the difficulties of the rural people and the way the tax collectors and other government officials exploited them. As his father was a government servant, politics was taboo in his house. However, in 1912, the emotional speeches of Hemanta Kumar, a student visitor from Calcutta (now Kolkata), who spoke on the citizens' duties to the Motherland, greatly influenced him.

After his spectacular success in the Matriculation examination Subhas was sent to Calcutta but he had already decided to pursue a meaningful life and contribute to the improvement of mankind. He joined the honours course in philosophy at Presidency College, Calcutta. He found genuine interest in his studies for the first time and western philosophy helped him develop a critical frame of mind and emancipated him from preconceived notions. He questioned the truth of the Vedanta on which he had taken his stand so long and wrote essays in defence of materialism, purely as an intellectual exercise. He came in conflict with the atmosphere of his group and it struck him for the first time that people were dogmatic in their views, taking certain things for granted. During the summer vacation of 1914, when he was just seventeen, he quietly left for a pilgrimage with a friend without informing anybody at home. He wanted to find a guru but failed. He practised ascetism to purify his character and develop self-discipline. A week's experience opened his eyes and unfolded a picture of the real India, the India of rampant illiteracy and villages where poverty stalked the land, and men died like flies. He realised that Yoga and other spiritual exercises were meaningless if they did not aim at promoting the well-being of the society.

Most of the college classes and lectures had very little interest for Subhas. He was slowly but steadily shedding his introvert character and taking greater interest in works of national reconstruction. In those days, the terrorist revolutionary movement had a peculiar fascination for the students of Bengal but Subhas and his group were more attracted to national reconstruction.

Often, on his way to and from college, Subhas passed through quarters inhabited by Englishmen and also met a large number of them in trams. Britishers on the trams were purposely rude and offensive to Indians in various ways. Subhas felt revolted by the behaviour of the British. The majority of the students of Presidency College were free thinkers. The college continued to be the storm centre and was looked upon by the British Government as a hot bed of sedition, a rendezvous of revolutionaries, and was frequently searched by the police. The first two years of his life were greatly influenced by the group which styled itself as the Neo-Vivekananda group and Subhas developed intellectually during this period. The group generally followed the teachings of Ramakrishna and Vivekananda with special emphasis on social service as the means to spiritual development.

Subhas graduated at the age of twenty-two and enrolled himself for a post-graduate course in experimental psychology as a special subject. His father, however, wanted him to go to England to appear for the Indian Civil Service. In spite of his reservations, Subhas took it as a challenge. In England, he was greatly impressed with the freedom allowed to students at Cambridge. Every student behaved in a dignified manner, and Subhas emulated them. He was of the view that Indians who go abroad must consider themselves to be the unofficial ambassadors who should uphold their country's prestige. Notwithstanding his preoccupation with his studies, he displayed his public spirit and fearlessness throughout his stay in England. He and K.L. Gouba were selected by the Indian Majlis to represent to the British Government, the difficulties the Indian students encountered for admission to the University Officers' Training Corps. Though he took a harsh view of the British highhandedness and racial arrogance, he did admire some of their qualities.

In July 1920, barely eight months after his arrival in England, Subhas appeared in the Civil Service Examination and passed it with distinction. But the prospect of being a member of the bureaucracy did not appeal to him. He felt that the first step towards equipping oneself for public service was to sacrifice all worldly interests. Much against the wishes of his father he resigned from the I.C.S. and returned to India. When C.R. Das became the chief organiser of the boycott of the visit of Prince of Wales, Subhas was by his side. The *hartal* in Calcutta was a spectacular success and both the guru and *shishya* found themselves in jail. This was Subhas's first incarceration, the first of a total of eleven. Later, when C.R. Das was elected Mayor of Calcutta, Subhas was appointed Chief Executive Officer. While holding this post he was arrested in a case of conspiracy and was sent to

Mandalay jail for two-and-a-half years without being tried. After being released from jail, he became President of the Bengal Pradesh Congress Committee and once again resumed his political activities.

Subhas became President of the All-India Youth Congress, General Officer Commanding of the Congress Volunteer Corps and, in 1928, was the co-founder, with Jawaharlal Nehru, of the Left wing of the Congress Party. He also became President of the All-India Trade Union Congress in 1931. His dynamism was a source of inspiration for trade unionists in the struggle for their rights as well as for India's freedom. In 1938, he was elected President of the Indian National Congress at the Haripura Session. This was the time when Congress ministries were in office in seven States under the scheme of Provincial Autonomy granted under the Government of India Act of 1935. He emphasised on the revolutionary potential of the Congress ministries in his presidential address. He was re-elected Congress President the following year at Tripuri, defeating the veteran Dr Pattabhai Sitaramayya though the latter enjoyed Mahatma Gandhi's support.

As Congress President, Subhas initiated the concept of planning in the organisation. He convened a meeting of Congress Ministers of Industries from the provinces at which it was decided to prepare a draft plan for the industrial development of the entire country to solve the problems of poverty and unemployment, of national defence and of economic regeneration in general. This was followed by the formation of the National Planning Committee in the Congress with Jawaharlal Nehru as its Chairman. In 1939, while Mahatma Gandhi and other leaders refused to do anything that might embarrass Britain during the War, Subhas determinedly pushed ahead for India's release from exploitation. He resolved to launch a struggle calling upon people not to help the imperialists with men, money or material. His study of history justified such an approach. He knew, for instance, that the fall of the Roman Empire had led to the emancipation of its colonies. He was arrested in July 1940 and kept under detention until December.

While in detention, Subhas had decided to leave India to seek foreign help and organise his own army to fight British imperialism. He confined himself to the room and visitors were severely restricted. On one night, he escaped and after an arduous journey he reached Peshawar on 19 January as Maulvi Ziauddin. From there he left for Kabul where an Indian businessman, Uttam Chand, helped him. He stayed in Kabul for nearly two months before he could secure help from the Italian Consul who arranged a meeting with the Italian Minister, Allberto Quaroni. At this meeting, it was planned that 50,000 men—Italian, German and Japanese—would reach the frontiers of India when the Indian army would desert, the masses would rise up and the end of English domination would be achieved in a very short time. His plan of precipitating a revolution and attacking the British power from outside, with an allied army of friendly anti-British powers, simultaneously, was appreciated by the Italian ministers.

Subhas reached Germany in the middle of the second year of the War. His arrival there was kept a closely guarded secret, though the Foreign Office there had this information through its office in Kabul. Hitler, at that time, did not have the least understanding either of India or of Indians. Therefore, it was felt that Germany could only give political asylum. Subhas was convinced that without proper military training and equipment, it was not possible for Indians outside to fight the British. He prepared an exhaustive plan for cooperation between the Axis Powers and India and submitted it to the

German Government. However, the Nazi officials wanted to impose certain conditions, which were not acceptable to Subhas and he left by submarine for South East Asia. Subhas felt that he could operate more effectively from a region closer to India. His arrival in Singapore sent India, and more particularly the political prisoners detained in the jails all over India, into ecstasy and optimism.

On 25 August, Subhas became the Supreme Commander of the *Azad Hind Fauj*, the Indian National Army, and proclaimed a Provisional Government of *Azad Hind* on 21 October. Thus, he was hailed by all, be they from the military or otherwise, as 'Netaji', the revered leader. 'I regard myself as the servant of thirty-eight crores of my countrymen,' he said. Japan, Germany and Italy accorded recognition to the provisional government and the entire country celebrated as if India had gained independence. Netaji came personally to the Andaman and Nicobar Islands, to liberate them. He re-named them as Shaheed and Swaraj islands, respectively, albeit temporarily. On 18 March 1944, after crossing the Burmese border, the Indian National Army stepped on Indian soil at Manipur where free India's banner was raised with the shouts of *'Jai Hind'* and *'Netaji zindabad'*. But before the INA's proposed advance to Imphal could materialise, torrential rain converted the region into a quagmire preventing mobility. The units had to fall back after a perilous journey. They retreated first to Mandalay, then to Rangoon and finally to Bangkok. There, they heard of Germany's defeat, and the bombing of Hiroshima and Nagasaki which culminated in the surrender of Japan.

Netaji's revolutionary spirit did not dampen even after Japan surrendered. 'Japan's surrender is not India's surrender,' he said. He knew that a war of liberation demanded great sacrifice, courage and patience. It was with his invincible spirit that Netaji opposed Wavell's offer and criticised the Congress leaders who were assessing it. The War was coming to a close with decisive Allied victory in almost all fronts. He was forced to leave Burma (now, Myanmar). On 17 August 1945, he issued a special order to the INA, which said, 'Delhi is still our goal.' He went to Singapore, then to Saigon from where he wanted to go to Russia. A special plane was arranged for him. In Russia, he wanted to seek Soviet help to fight the British. He was to fly to Dairen first via Taipei. But the ill-fated plane crashed in Taipei on 18 August 1945, on its way to Dairen, resulting in his death. Some people believe that the news was not correct and he is still alive.

Thereafter, the nation faced the historic trial of the three INA heroes: Captain Shah Nawaz Khan, Captain P.K. Sehgal and Lieutenant Gurbaksh Singh Dhillon. The first was a Muslim, the second a Hindu and the third a Sikh, symbolising the secular and integrated character of the INA and, indeed, of India itself. The defence led by Bhulabhai Desai, Jawaharlal Nehru and K.N. Katju formed one of the most glorious chapters of India's' politico-legal history. The historic trial in Delhi's Red Fort has been described as a fitting commemoration of the role of Subhas Chandra Bose in India's freedom struggle.

About two decades later, at a function when relics of Netaji were presented to the nation, the then President, Dr Zakir Husain observed: 'It was a historic campaign—a military campaign no doubt, but it was not waged for territorial aggrandisement or for subjugation of other people. It was a revolutionary struggle, which Netaji carried out, with undaunted courage and crusading zeal in the most hazardous circumstances for achieving the freedom of his motherland. Today, after more than four decades we miss his magical presence, ennobling words and dedication to the cause of the Motherland.'

Shyama Prasad Mookerji

*D*r Shyama Prasad Mookerji was one of the many remarkable figures who adorned India's political firmament during the crucial decades before and after Independence. Blessed with an elegant personality, brilliant intellect, impeccable character, robust self-confidence, and a deep sense of patriotism, he excelled in whatever field of activity he entered—as the acting president of the Hindu Mahasabha, or as parliamentarian, or even the first president of the Jana Sangh, now Bharatiya Janata Party (BJP). He made his mark as a dynamic and clear-headed politician when he ousted the Muslim League Ministry of Bengal and installed a coalition government under the leadership of Fazal-ul-Haq.

Born on 7 July 1901 in Calcutta (now Kolkata), Shyama Prasad Mookerji was the second son of Sir Ashutosh Mookerji, former Vice-Chancellor of Calcutta University and judge of the Calcutta High Court. He was a very knowledgeable, extremely well-educated and well-read man. He was held in great esteem by his contemporaries. Shyama Prasad inherited many of the qualities of Sir Ashutosh by birth and others he acquired through his example and worthy guidance. The most noteworthy of these qualities, which had made Sir Ashutosh the idol of his people, were his robust uncompromising nationalism and his fearlessness.

Shyama Prasad spent his childhood in Bhawanipur, then a suburb of Calcutta. His house was the meeting place of great intellectuals, jurists, politicians and statesmen of Bengal and India. Sir Ashutosh had filled it with books on all subjects and a look at the variety and quality of the books gave one an idea of the versatility and rare understanding of the sciences and humanities alike, which distinguished Sir Ashutosh and his son Shyama Prasad had. This house was also well-known to the people around for the pomp and show, devotion and piety, with which *poojas* were celebrated year after year. Young Shyama Prasad saw and imbibed with reverence the spirit of both these aspects of his family. He also listened to discussions on the most modern and scientific subjects between his father and great scholars who visited their house from time to time from all parts of India and abroad. He developed a deep sense of respect for both India's age-old culture and thought, together with a deep attachment to western thought and learning born out of intellectual understanding. His mind was thus a healthy blend of Hindu spirituality, the ideals of tolerance and humanity, as well as the scientific outlook and broad understanding of the West.

Shyama Prasad was a voracious reader. While still in school he read several books prescribed for college and university level students. Sir Ashutosh involved his son in his daily affairs, often dictating letters which Shyama Prasad wrote in long hand to be typed later. Sir Ashutosh also began to take him to Calcutta University which gave the boy an opportunity to interact with university professors.

Shyama Prasad passed his matriculation examination at the age of sixteen from the Mitter Institute with a scholarship and joined Presidency College in 1917. He could now feel his father's influence in shaping the educational life of Bengal. It provided him new opportunities to assist his father in his educational work, and gain insight into the affairs of Calcutta University. Like his father, he chose the *dhoti* and *kurta* in preference to the European dress as his normal attire.

In 1919, Shyama Prasad passed his Inter-Arts examination with the highest marks. This established his reputation as a student and he was appointed General Secretary of the Presidency College Magazine in 1920. The editorship of the college magazine provided him an opportunity for self-expression. In College, Shyama Prasad developed a special taste for English literature. In 1921, he stood first in the Bachelor of Arts examination with honours in English. He would have taken this subject for his Master of Arts degree also, but his father' struggle to give Bengali and other vernaculars their rightful place in the educational curricula of Calcutta University influenced his decision. Therefore, he chose Bengali and passed the examination again in first class in 1923. In 1924, he appeared for the Bachelor of Law examination, once again standing first in the university and was enrolled as an advocate of the Calcutta High Court. During the year 1923–24, he regularly contributed articles to *Capital*, edited by Pat Lovell under the pen-name of 'Dutch'. By writing for these journals, he developed a fascinating style, both in Bengali and English.

In 1922, while Shyama Prasad was still preparing for his master's degree, he was married to Sudha Devi, who bore him four children: two sons and two daughters. She died in 1934.

Shyama Prasad was in Calcutta University for fifteen years. There, he established his reputation as an original thinker and brilliant educationist. He was respected as one of the foremost educationists in the country. He worked in the university in various capacities, as president of the councils of post-graduate studies in art and science, dean of the faculty of arts and vice-chancellor. Even though he was the youngest fellow of the country's premier university, his intimate knowledge of the subject gave him an unprecedented position in its affairs. He could be depended upon for all important matters. He was only twenty-four at that time. He had a keen desire to complete his legal studies in England.

In March 1926, Shyama Prasad went to England and joined Lincoln's Inn and was called to the English Bar in 1927. While in England, he represented Calcutta University at the Conference of the Universities of the British Empire. It was in England that Shyama Prasad came in close contact with Dr S. Radhakrishnan and Sir Evans Greaves. He was known to be a quiet and unostentatious kind of student by his contemporaries in England. But his amiable nature won him a large number of friends.

Shyama Prasad returned to India in 1927 and pursued a legal practice for some time. But his preoccupation with the university soon forced him to take up public and educational work. He was elected to the Bengal Legislative Council as a Congress candidate representing Calcutta University in 1929. In 1930, he resigned his seat in the council when the Congress decided to boycott the legislatures. When he found it necessary that the interests of the university be safeguarded in the legislatures, he sought re-election and returned once again in 1930 as an independent member representing Calcutta University. His main concern was the cause of education.

In 1934, Shyama Prasad was appointed Vice-Chancellor of Calcutta University. He was only thirty-three at that time, the youngest vice-chancellor of any university in the country. He had lost his wife just a year earlier and his mother, to whom he was devotedly attached, tried her best to persuade him to marry again. But he refused. He decided to dedicate the rest of his life to the service of his motherland. The vice-chancellorship of Calcutta University gave him the opportunity to put his aims and ideals for his people in practice. As vice-chancellor he was keen to re-model the syllabi and courses and re-organise the training and examination system to ensure that the learner may not grow up as a mechanised recorder of information and theories but with strengthened critical judgement. 'Our ideal', he said, 'is to provide extensive facilities for education from the lowest grade to the highest, to mould our educational purpose and to draw out the best qualities that are hidden in our youth and to train them intellectually and physically for devoted service in all spheres of national activity, in villages, in towns and cities.'

He was keen to link up education with the best elements of our culture and civilisation, drawing strength, wherever necessary from the fountain of western skill and knowledge. He pursued this ideal in a systematic way during the four years of his vice-chancellorship. He gave due status to Bengali and other vernacular languages in the curricula of the university. Bengali was made the medium of instruction up to matriculation, and he introduced Honours courses in Bengali, Hindi and Urdu. To prepare textbooks in Bengali, he had a collection of technical terms and expressions in Bengali prepared to be used in various subjects of study. The university undertook the publication of a special series of Bengali books on different branches of knowledge. The usage of Bengali spelling was also standardised on his initiative.

He introduced the system of compartmental examinations and gave concession to students who had failed to appear in examinations without getting themselves admitted into colleges. A variety of courses and combinations were introduced for the boys and alternative subjects and courses of study were prescribed for the girls. A Teachers' Training Department at Calcutta University was organised and short-term training courses, including vocational course, were provided for trained teachers for schools. In order to create a feeling of brotherhood among the reserved hostels for the students coming from the backward classes, the reservation system was abolished and all of them were provided accommodation in general hostels. Messes were attached to the colleges at reduced rates. Students' Appointment Board gave guidance to the students about choice of careers. Shyama Prasad took keen interest in finding employment for the educated youth among whom unemployment was growing rapidly. He gave greater attention to technical and scientific studies. Schemes for agricultural education and diploma course in education were introduced. He also initiated a scheme for imparting training in the large-scale production of certain industrial goods in the Applied Chemistry Department of the University.

Shyama Prasad was elected a member of the Court and Council of the Indian Institute of Sciences, Bangalore, as a representative of the Universities of Eastern India. He also became a Chairman of the Inter-University Board. Calcutta University conferred on him the degree of Honorary Doctor of Laws at a special convocation held in November 1938. His term as vice-chancellor ended in 1938.

Education broadened his mind and created political consciousness, arousing his desire for emancipation from the colonial regime. Being a member of the Bengal Legislative Council, as well as a Congress candidate, had already given him an insight into politics. The Congress attitude towards the Communal Award came as a great shock to him. It shook his faith in that organisation. The introduction in 1937 of the provincial part of the Government of India Act of 1935 and the elections to the Provincial Legislatures during this year created a new situation. He was again elected to the Bengal Assembly from the University constituency and had an opportunity to study the working of provincial autonomy minutely. The Congress' handling of the situation in and outside the legislature soon provoked him to think afresh about its policies and political conceptions. Politics demanded his alignment with one or the other recognised political parties of the country which might provide him with a popular base. The Indian National Congress, the most powerful political organisation in the country, with which he had been associated since his entry into public life, would have been his natural choice but the experience that he had gained of its philosophy and ideals, both in theory and practice, in and outside the legislatures, disillusioned him. He found it worthwhile to ally with Vinayak Damodar Savarkar who had infused new life into Hindu Mahasabha within a few months and had come to Calcutta to re-organise the Mahasabha movement in Bengal.

Dr Mookerji was much impressed by Veer Savarkar's analysis of the Indian political situation and his gospel of unalloyed nationalism as the only effective antidote to Muslim separatism and divide-and-rule policy of the alien rulers. He found it a practical and realistic approach to the problems posed by the Muslim League in Bengal and elsewhere. He, therefore, decided to join the Hindu Mahasabha and make it an effective instrument for checkmating the anti-national policies of the Muslim League and the 'cowardly' passivity of the Congress. He took leading part in the annual session of the All India Hindu Mahasabha held in Calcutta. Soon after, he became its acting president due to Savarkar's continued ill-health. The entry of Dr Mookerji into the Hindu Mahasabha and his quick rise to the position of its acting president marked the beginning of his active political career. His intellectual attainments, dauntless spirit, moral fibre, and power of elocution made him a welcome addition to the political arena.

Dr Mookerji's contributions to the Hindu Mahasabha galvanised the Bengal unit of the Mahasabha into a dynamic and growing organisation. His bold but rational presentation of Mahasabha ideology and his frontal attack on the Congress policy of appeasement of and compromise with the Muslim League and other anti-national forces at the cost of the Hindus and to the detriment of the wider interests of the country, created a stir all over Bengal and India. He toured the whole of India, addressed mammoth gatherings and left his impresson on all those who came in contact with him. His exposition was so forceful, so methodical and convincing that he set all his listeners thinking. In Lahore, he addressed a rally of the Rashtriya Swayamsevak Sangh (RSS) as well. He saw in this organisation the one silver lining in the cloudy sky of India and this drew him closer to it in his later years. His whirlwind tour took the country by storm. His personality gave to the Mahasabha a new status and prestige and he himself became an all-India figure.

Dr Mookerji joined the coalition ministry in Bengal. The governor and the British bureaucracy were openly hostile to the new ministry. They were upset with their failure to have a Muslim League ministry and wanted the coalition government to fall. Dr Mookerji's stature as an educationist and leader of the intellectual elite of Bengal forced the governor to show him deference whether he liked it or not. Soon, he was looked upon as the brain and guiding spirit of the coalition ministry. Within a few days of his becoming a minister, he asserted his dauntless spirit and conviction of courage, but he resigned when he found the failure of the Cripps Mission which had made the prospect of a negotiated settlement between the government and the people of India remote. He disapproved of the policy adopted by the British Government of India with regard to the prevailing political situation in the country.

His exit from the Bengal Cabinet immediately brought Dr Mookerji into the wider all-India stage. The food situation in Bengal soon compelled the humanitarian in him to concentrate his attention on devising ways and means to relieve the distress of the famine-stricken people. It became so grave that thousands of people from the villages began to trek to cities after disposing of all their cattle and chattels in search of food. Even in cities, the price of rice had risen so high that most of the middle-class families with fixed incomes were finding it difficult to get two square meals. Dr Mookerji organised large-scale relief operations. The Hindu Mahasabha Relief Committee was formed which then coordinated with the Arya Samaj, the Marwari Society and the Ramakrishna Mission. The whole country from Assam to Kanyakumari responded magnificently to Dr Mookerji's call.

When Dr Mookerji found the Anglo-Muslim game of destroying the age-old unity of the country, he called attention to this new danger and sounded a note of warning to all concerned at the 25th Annual Session of the Hindu Mahasabha, held at Amritsar in December 1943. In the absence of Veer Savarkar, Dr Mookerji presided over the historic session of the Mahasabha. His presidential address gave a clear exposition of his political philosophy and his stand regarding the demand for partition. He said that the only solution to India's problems was to rigidly exclude all extraneous considerations based on caste and religion from the field of politics. His approach to the communal problem was absolutely rational and national. The district magistrate banned the presidential procession just at the eleventh hour. The Reception Committee lacked the courage to defy the order and decided to cancel the procession. The Hindu Mahasabha never recovered from this setback and fell in popular estimation.

In 1944, Dr Mookerji started an English daily, *The Nationalist*, which soon became a powerful organ for moulding public opinion. He participated in the Constituent Assembly of India where his political acumen, oratorial skill, and mastery of parliamentary procedure won him laurels. After the Partition, Mahatma Gandhi felt that freedom had been achieved by the combined efforts of all the nationalist forces in the country and not by the Congress alone. He wanted the first government of free India to be a national government capable of inspiring confidence and creating enthusiasm in the whole nation. He, therefore, insisted that the first cabinet should be broad-based. It was on his insistence that a number of distinguished non-Congressmen were also invited to join the cabinet. They included Sir John Mathai, the noted economist and business magnate; Sir Shanmukham Chetty, the well-known financial expert; and Dr B.R. Ambedkar, a celebrated jurist and leader of the scheduled castes. Dr Mookerji was also invited. Though he would have personally preferred education, he was given the portfolio of industry and supply. It gave him an opportunity to lay the foundation of India's industrial policy and prepare the ground for the industrial development of the country in years to come. He had very clear ideas on the role of private capital in the industrial development of the country as also on the relationship between capital and labour.

Dr Mookerji differed with Prime Minister Jawaharlal Nehru on the problem of India's relations and dealings with Pakistan, particularly in regard to the condition of the Hindu minority in East Bengal. He felt that the Government of India had failed to name Pakistan as an aggressor, even after the fact of her aggression in Kashmir had been fully established and the forced payment of fifty-five crore rupees to Pakistan under pressure of Mahatma Gandhi's fast pained him and convinced him of the imbecility of the government of which he himself was a member. He instinctively felt that this policy would only encourage Pakistan. He was deeply concerned with the issue of Hindus in East Pakistan. Dr Mookerji urged upon Nehru and his other colleagues to remember the pledges they had given to them and to do something for their safety. The result was the first Inter-Dominion agreement signed at Calcutta in April 1948 which dealt mainly with the question of minorities in the two Bengals. This agreement, however, failed to produce lasting results. But the exodus of Hindus from East Bengal continued unabated. There were numerous conferences of officials from both sides and copious correspondence was exchanged between the two governments, but judged by actual results, Pakistan's attitude continued to remain unchanged. The worst came early in 1950 when the Muslims started a large-scale massacre of Hindus all over the province. More than fifty thousand Hindus were butchered, thousands of Hindu women were abducted and raped and inhuman and most barbarous crimes were perpetrated against them.

Angered by the government and hurt by the tragedy Dr Mookerji walked out of the exalted position he had held in the government for two-and-a-half years. He submitted his resignation on 1 April 1950. He now started working to create a political platform through which Indian nationalism might project and assert itself and checkmate the government's policies. He now wanted the Hindu Mahasabha to make the world realise the true import of the word 'Hindu' and take up the task of Hinduising—politically, socially as well as culturally—those elements in the country which had been misled by British propaganda and the Congress 'folly to detest their own national name and ideals and play the role of disruptionists'. The Muslim problem, he felt convinced, 'could be solved in free India, once and for all, if their outlook on cultural, social and political problems of the country was Hinduised or nationalised while leaving them free, in keeping with the Hindu tradition of absolute tolerance, to carry on their religion and way of worship as they pleased'.

But following the assassination of Mahatma Gandhi on 30 January 1948 the Congress Party 'exploited the situation to suppress all its real or imaginary, actual or potential rivals'. The workers of the RSS were arrested and detained without trial. Some of the Mahasabha leaders were also arrested and the existence of the Mahasabha came to be threatened. It decided to suspend its political activities. In 1949, the ban on the RSS was lifted and in August 1949 the Mahasabha also resumed its activities. But Dr Mookerji had some differences and resigned from its executive. He wanted the Mahasabha to grow with the times and admit members irrespective of their religion or caste. He left it when he found that it had lost the will and strength to grow.

By that time, RSS had established its name on the national scene. Dr Mookerji had already come into contact with the founder and leader of this movement, Dr Keshar Baliram Hedgewar, in the mid-1930s at Calcutta. In 1940, he had described it as the 'only silver lining in the cloudy sky of India'. The good work done by its *swayamsevaks* in the Punjab, Kashmir, NWFP and Sind in 1947, their self-immolation in the cause of their country and its people and the bravery and strength they had exhibited against the brutal and violent attacks of the Pakistanis had won his unqualified praise and respect. But the RSS was, till then, a non-political organisation, devoted exclusively to the work of character building, cultural upliftment, social cohesion, and awakening of true national consciousness amongst the people in general. There was, therefore, an urgent need for a political organisation which could reflect the ideology and ideas of the RSS in the political sphere. With this in view, the All-India Bharatiya Jana Sangh was launched in 1951 with Dr Shyama Prasad Mookerji as its President.

The Bharatiya Jana Sangh came into existence on the eve of the first general elections held under the provision of the new Constitution of free India. The party had neither the resources nor as yet the organisation to ensure for him the minimum of comforts and fast means of transportation. But Dr Mookerji had faith in India's destiny and confidence in himself. In the course of his tours across the length and breadth of the country during those election months, he had the opportunity to watch from close quarters the men, young and old, who constituted the Jana Sangh at the town, district and provincial levels. But, in spite of this, only three of its candidates, including Dr Mookerji and Barrister U.M. Trivedi out of the ninety-three, who contested on its ticket for the Lok Sabha, were elected. In the various States, it had put up 1,742 candidates out of which only thirty-three were elected. In some provinces like the East Punjab, where Jana Sangh appeared to be the strongest, it could not secure a single seat. The inexperience of the young workers for whom elections were a novel experience and the lack of resources accounted for this failure to a great extent.

Dr Mookerji was not in favour of allowing a separate status to Jammu and Kashmir. In order to accomplish this he entered Jammu and Kashmir without securing permit in May 1953. He was arrested at Kathua under the Public Safety

Act of the State even though he had been allowed to proceed to the State without permit by the Government of India. He was taken to Srinagar where he was lodged in Srinagar Central Jail. There, on 23 June he died under mysterious circumstances.

In spite of his total pre-occupation with politics, Dr Mookerji had developed a keen interest and devotion to education, culture and the moral and spiritual values the country stood for. For him 'culture' or '*sanskriti*' meant the sum total of the highest achievements of the people in the realm of thought and action which imperceptibly mould the mind and influence the conduct of people, individually as well as collectively. History, literature, lives of great men and national festivals, he held, play a great part in this process of influencing the conduct of a race. He considered Indian culture to be in essence Hindu culture which grew from the Vedic times, absorbing and assimilating the contributions of a number of new elements which, in the course of history, got merged into Hindu society. Dr Mookerji believed that men like Swami Vivekananda and Lala Hardayal had done more to raise the stock of India in the eyes of the West than all the political missions that India had sent out since her freedom. He looked upon Buddha as a world teacher who gave the best of Indian thought and culture to the world through his life and teachings. With his passing away India lost a valuable cultural ambassador and a great political leader.

Chandra Shekhar Azad

Chandra Shekhar Azad became a martyr at the age of twenty-four in the historic struggle of Indian independence. In his quest for freedom he was joined by revolutionaries like Bhagat Singh, Rajguru, Sukhdev, Bhagwati Charan, Saligram Shukla, Batukeshwar Dutt, Bejoy Kumar Sinha, Siya Verma and Sadashiv Rao.

Chandra Shekhar was born on 23 July 1906 in Bhavra village in the Jhabua district in Madhya Pradesh. He was the son of Pandit Sitaram Tiwari, a watchman in the royal gardens. Sita Ram was a native of Badarka in the district of Unnao in modern Uttar Pradesh. He had to leave his ancestral house in search of living and finally settled in Bhavra. As a child, Chandra Shekhar spent his days among the Bhil boys. Once, while celebrating Diwali with some tribal children, he held a bunch of flaming matchsticks in his hand. As the matchsticks burnt, he told his tribal friends: 'Look, this is how you should learn to bear pain.'

The boy went to the local village school, but more than the books, he was interested in running along brooks, climbing trees, and playing with the cattle. He was good at wrestling and archery. After completing his primary education, Chandra Shekhar went to Benaras, learnt Sanskrit and studied the *Shastras* (scriptures). When he was fourteen, he was arrested by the police for taking part in the Non-cooperation movement. When the British magistrate asked his name, his father's name and his residential address, he replied that his name was Azad (independent), his father's name was *Swatantra* (independence) and his residence was prison. The magistrate was furious and ordered for him fifteen lashes of flogging. A special whip was brought. Chandra Shekhar was stripped to the skin and then tied to the flogging triangle. It was a public flogging, a concept the Britishers had introduced during the Jallianwalla Bagh massacre. With every new lash the rebel shouted: *Vande mataram, Mahatma Gandhi ki jai, Bharat Mata ki jai.* Even when his skin was torn and he was bleeding profusely he kept raising slogans in praise of freedom and his Motherland. His endurance stunned his captor. At the end of the fifteenth cane lash, three *annas* (fraction of a rupee, the then Indian currency) were placed on Chandra Shekhar's palm according to the rules of the prison. But he had the audacity to throw the three coins back to the jailor and stand defiant like a wounded lion. Through his act of defiance, he endeared himself to the people. It was at this stage that he was hailed as '*Azad*' and the name stuck.

When the non-violent Non-cooperation Movement was withdrawn, he became restless and was slowly drawn towards the revolutionary movement. Benaras, at that time, was the stronghold of the movement. He came in contact with Manmath Nath Gupta, Pranvesh Chatterji and others and became a member of the *Hindustan Prajatantra Sangh* (the Hindustan Republican Association).

Chandra Shekhar's qualities of leadership were immediately recognised and he became the Commander-in-Chief of the Army of the Republican Association.

In 1924, Azad was made the head of the Uttar Pradesh unit of the association. In a short time, he became a terror to the British police and the hero of the people. At a meeting in September 1928, a new collective leadership adopted socialism as their goal and changed their party's name to the Hindustan Socialist Republican Association. Its object was to establish a republic of the States of India by an organised and armed revolution. Collection of money and arms was made mandatory. For this purpose, in some circumstances, it was deemed proper to resort even to assassination. Chandra Shekhar was in the forefront in every armed action.

The first armed action towards this end in view was the Kakori Train hold-up, which took place on 9 August 1925. The plot was devised by Chandra Shekhar with the help of Ram Prasad Bismal. Ten young men who boarded the train at Kakori railway station, which was proceeding to Alamnagar in Saharanpur-Lucknow sector, seized the government treasury. The British police somehow came to know of the plot and arrested Ram Prasad, Ashfaqullah, Roshan Singh and Lahiri who were consequently hanged. But Chandra Shekhar could not be apprehended.

After this incident, Chandra Shekhar shifted to Jhansi, where he lived and worked for the Bundelkhand Motor Company as a mechanic under the assumed name of Hari Shankar, all the while continuing his activities as a revolutionary. One of his neighbours, Ram Dayal often got drunk at night and beat his wife. One da, Chandra Shekhar asked Ram Dayal to stop beating his wife. Ram Dayal abused Chandra Shekhar, and called him 'saala' (wife's brother, though used as a derogatory word used for a mean person). 'Now, if you beat her I am bound to save my sister,' said Chandra Shekhar. In a drunken state, Ram Dayal beat his wife again, dragging her by her hair and abusing her. True to his word Chandra Shekhar intervened and thrashed Ram Dayal repeatedly till he realised his mistake and pledged not to beat his wife again.

Once Chandra Shekhar came across a Pathan thrashing a labourer who had not paid back his loan in time. Chandra Shekhar stopped him and said: 'Khan Baba, give him some time and he will pay your money back.' But Khan did not like the intervention and warned Chandra Shekhar to keep away. At this, Chandra Shekhar pounced on the Pathan and did not let him go till he begged for mercy. After this incident, the children of the locality started calling Azad 'Lion' and people began coming to him for help. The police in Jhansi got suspicious. When Azad found that the police had come to know, he slipped off to Orchha, constructed a hut on the banks of a river and started living there.

These two instances show the innate feelings of Chandra Shekhar. He could never tolerate injustice against any person. He rebelled against the person or society perpetrating uncalled for violence thus harming any person with personal motive.

In 1928, the Hindustan Socialist Republican Association decided to hold a black flag demonstration at Lahore on 30 October 1928 to protest against the impending visit of the Simon Commission, which did not include a single Indian. Azad joined this peaceful demonstration along with Punjab Kesri Lala Lajpat Rai, Bhagat Singh, and many other revolutionaries. The British police, for whom Lala Lajpat Rai had become a scare, pounced on him without any provocation. Though Lala Lajpat Rai looked frail his spirit was dauntless. *Lathis* (canes) were hurled on him but he stood like a rock, not permitting his people to hit back. The Superintendent of Police, Scott, personally conducted the operation in Lahore. In the face of such atrocities Lala Lajpat Rai said: 'Every blow that they hurled at us will drive a nail in the coffin of the British empire.' Eighteen days after this incident, on 17 November 1928, Lala Lajpat Rai succumbed to his injuries.

The Hindustan Socialist Republication Association attributed this as a national humiliation. Several meetings were held and it was decided to avenge the death of Lala Lajpat Rai. Chander Shekhar, Rajguru and Bhagat Singh were deputed for the task. On the appointed day, Bhagat Singh and Rajguru waited outside the office of the police superintendent. As soon as an Englishman in uniform came out of the office, Rajguru fired the first shot at an officer who turned out to be J.P. Saunders, Assistant Superintendent of Police instead of Scott. The bullet hit Saunders on his forehead and he fell down. Bhagat Singh moved ahead and fired four more shots and Saunders died instantly. Azad killed Channan Singh, a head constable, who tried to chase them with a single shot. Next day, people saw posters throughout Lahore announcing that Lala Lajpat Rai's death had been avenged.

Bhagat Singh and Rajguru got shelter in a house. Azad sought asylum in a house, which turned out to be the house of a freedom fighter's widow. The woman was worried about the marriage of her daughter but had no money. The police had announced a reward of Rs 10,000 for information regarding Chandra Shekhar Azad's whereabouts. Seeing the plight of the woman Azad told her to inform the police, get this money and fix the marriage. The lady got enraged and reprimanded Azad for his 'foolish' offer saying, 'My daughter can remain unmarried but I cannot bear the stigma of being a traitor. I'm a freedom fighter's widow and I will hold aloft the flag of freedom.' It is said that Chandra Shekhar Azad slipped away that night leaving a bundle of money amounting to ten thousand rupees. He then headed towards the house of Durga Bhabhi, wife of Professor Bhagvati Charan Vohra, who wielded tremendous influence on the revolutionaries.

She suggested that they escape to Calcutta. Azad sat in a third class compartment disguised as a *sadhu* singing the *dohas* of Tulsidas. Bhagat Singh travelled with Durga Bhabhi as her husband while Rajguru, their 'servant', sat in the servant's compartment.

Chandra Shekhar Azad was given the responsibility of planning a plot to throw a live bomb in the Central Assembly at Delhi. The job was allotted to Bhagat Singh and Batukeshwar Dutt. On 8 April 1929, two bombs were thrown in such a manner that no one was killed. Only four members were hurt slightly and that too as a result of the commotion caused. A red pamphlet was also thrown on the floor of the House, where the bomb was not intended to kill anyone. Its purpose was only to awaken the administration. After this incident, Bhagat Singh and Dutt volunteered arrest while Azad escaped.

In his next move, Chandra Shekhar Azad resolved to blow up the train by which the Viceroy was travelling. The duty was assigned to Yash Pal in December 1929. The explosion took place near the Purana Qila railway track in Delhi. But the Viceroy had a providential escape. However, the special train was damaged. On 6 July 1930, Azad masterminded an armed robbery and robbed a Delhi firm of Rs 14,000. With most of his comrades either in prison or dead, he was left alone to fight the might of the British Empire. To hoodwink the British police, at times, he worked in Punjab as a motor-driver, a cook, a boatman or a mechanic. He even planned to free Bhagat Singh from the Lahore central jail on the day he was to be taken to the court. But the government decided to have the military court inside the jail.

In February 1931, Chandra Shekhar Azad held discussions in Alfred Park, Allahabad, where he planned a mass revolution on the lines of the Bolshevik revolution in Russia. On 27 February 1931, the police came to know that Azad was meeting with his associate Sukhdev Raj. The police superintendent fired at Azad, hitting his thigh. He remained conscious and hid himself behind a tree. From there, he fired back. The bullet injured the police superintendent's wrist. Azad fought like a lion when the other policemen surrounded him. The police rained bullets on him from all sides, but Azad kept on firing back at them. When only one bullet was left with him, he placed the gun against his temple, fired the last shot and fell dead, living to his resolve never to be caught and dragged to the gallows and hanged. Four bullets and a part of a fifth were extracted from his body as per post-mortem report. He was cremated at Rasulabad Ghat under a heavy police guard.

Chandra Shekhar Azad's indomitable will and resilience against the British endeared him to Indians in his time and after. This spirit and patriotism have earned him a place in the annals of Indian history as one of the greatest freedom fighters of all times.

Bhagat Singh

Bhagat Singh was a key player in the struggle for Indian independence from British rule. His energy and charisma proved a potential challenge to the British Raj and the popularity he achieved was amazing. He was dauntless in the face of death, determined to smash imperialist rule and raise on its ruins the edifice of free India. His virility, his style and way of living, his writings, statements, speeches and acts of defiance against the British Raj made him into a colourful legend and a role model.

Born on 27 September 1907 in Banga in Punjab, Bhagat Singh was the son of Kishan Singh and Vidyawati. He was born into a family with glorious revolutionary traditions. His grandfather was the first to set the ball rolling by showing an inclination towards the ideals of the Arya Samaj after meeting Swami Dayanand, even though he was a Jat Sikh. His grandfather, Arjun Singh's involvement with the Arya Samaj only shows that he was open to new ideas. He got his sons, Kishan Singh and Ajit Singh admitted to the Saindas Anglo-Sanskrit School. Bhagat Singh's father was also involved in revolutionary activities. The day Bhagat Singh was born his father and his uncles were released from Lahore Central Jail and Mandalay simultaneously. All these strange coincidences held great joy for the family which decided to name the child 'Bhagwanwala', who heralded luck to the family.

Bhagat Singh's father, Kishan Singh, and his uncle, Ajit Singh, were Amritdhari sikhs. They were inspired by Guru Gobind Singh's great sacrifices. Their love for the motherland and obsession to ensure its emancipation from the British rule turned them into revolutionaries. The social and political consciousness in Punjab, which had earlier begun with Guru Nanak and was consolidated as a sense of nationalism with the coming of Guru Nanak, gradually spread to other parts of the country. The Akali wave in Punjab, the Arya Samaj movement, the struggle of the Indian National Congress, and the Kirti Kisan movement were vital ingredients of reformism and militancy.

Ajit Singh's wife, Harnam Kaur—Bhagat Singh's aunt—would often take the boy in her lap and recount to him the exploits and adventures of his forefathers. Listening to the tortures and agony inflicted by the British on his forefathers had a profound effect on the young boy.

Right from his childhood, Bhagat Singh seemed to have prepared himself to meet British violence with violence. The boy had a streak of seriousness in his temperament. When he was in the fourth class, he had already read books by his uncle Ajit Singh, Sufi Amba Prasad and Lala Hardyal. Literature on the world's revolutionary movements was available to him in his home. As a child, he kept the company of revolutionaries like Mehta Anand Kishore, Lala Pindi Das and Sufi Amba Prasad. Under the influence of all such persons he had turned on to the path to the freedom struggle. He was greatly influenced by *Koma Gata Maru*. The hanging of his nineteen-year-old friend, Kartar Singh, in the Lahore Conspiracy Case had a profound effect on the nine-year-old Bhagat Singh.

In 1917, when his office transferred Bhagat Singh's father to Lahore, the boy joined D.A.V. Middle School. When the tragic Jallianwala Bagh incident took place on 13 April 1919, Bhagat Singh reached Amritsar and made obeisance to the blood-drenched earth and brought with him some of the earth to Lahore in a jar. He swore to avenge the victims of the massacre with blood. In August 1921, when Mahatma Gandhi began his Non-cooperation movement, Bhagat Singh left school while in ninth class and joined the movement. But after some time he joined the National College, Lahore. Bhai Parmanand and Lala Lajpat Rai established this college for those who had left their institutions to join the Non-cooperation movement. Vidya Alankar, Bhagat Singh's history professor, left a profound impression on him. He studied the history of revolutionaries and social movements of the world.

In 1924, when Bhagat Singh's mother was planning his marriage, he left home and arrived at Kanpur to join the revolutionary activities. There he met Ganesh Shankar Vidyarthi. He joined Pratap Press and changed his name to Balwant Singh. In his leisure time, Bhagat Singh read the history of revolutions in different countries and about communism. He became a member of the Hindustan Republican Association. As a member of the association, he went to villages in Uttar Pradesh to distribute books and leaflets about revolutionaries. The young men in schools and colleges, workers and peasants were educated on violent revolution. Ganesh Shankar Vidyarthi was impressed with Bhagat Singh's courage and capacity for revolutionary work. It was through Vidyarthi's influence that Bhagat Singh was appointed Headmaster in the National School of Shadipur in Aligarh district in northern India. There, he instilled in the students a love for the nation and encouraged them to work for its independence.

Six months had elapsed since Bhagat Singh left Lahore. His family had no inkling of his whereabouts. His grandmother became very ill and he returned to Lahore. But in 1925, he had to leave for Kanpur in connection with the Kakori Dacoity Case to help members of the Hindustan Socialist Association escape from jail.

On 30 October 1928, a large rally was organised to protest against the members of the Simon Commission. Lala Lajpat Rai and Bhagat Singh led the procession. A large number of people were injured in the *lathi*-charge. Lala Lajpat Rai was seriously injured and later succumbed to his injuries. The death of Lala Lajpat Rai was a great loss to Bhagat Singh who itched to answer British violence with violence. Sukh Dev, Raj Guru, Chander Shekhar Azad and Jai Gopal joined him.

Bhagat Singh and Sukh Dev slipped from Lahore to Amritsar. Here, they met some revolutionaries and set up a bomb-making factory in Agra with branches in Lahore and Saharanpur. They decided to throw bombs in the Assembly when the Public Safety Bill and the Trader Disputes Bill were being presented. After throwing the bombs Bhagat Singh and B.K. Dutt stood still. There was no fear on their faces. They were arrested and they confessed to having thrown the bombs. In a statement made by them jointly before the judge they stated that 'The bomb was necessary to awaken England from her dreams.' They said that they were inspired by the ideals, which guided Guru Gobind Singh and Shivaji and held human life sacred beyond words. When asked in the lower court what he meant by revolution, Bhagat Singh replied that revolution doesn't necessarily involve sanguinary strife nor is there any place in it for individual vendetta. By revolution he meant that the 'present' order of things, which was based on manifest injustice, must change. By revolution he also meant the ultimate establishment of an order of society. At the altar of this revolution, he and his associates had brought their youth as an incense, for no sacrifice to them was too great for so magnificent a cause.

The session judge dismissed the statement of Bhagat Singh and B.K. Dutt and sentenced them to transportation for life. When they appealed to the High Court, the High Court endorsed the decision of the sessions judge on 13 January 1930. While in jail, Bhagat Singh met the old revolutionaries of the Ghadar Movement. When he saw that the political prisoners were being badly treated, he launched a jails reform movement and organised hunger strikes. The authorities were forced to yield and a Jail Inquiry Committee was constituted. When the Committee recommended a number of facilities, they ended their strike.

On 10 July 1929, the Lahore Conspiracy case came up for hearing before a special magistrate in the jail itself. When Bhagat Singh reached the court, slogans like 'Inquilab zindabad' electrified the atmosphere. He started by reciting a poem of the revolutionary Om Prakash: 'Kabhi woh din bhi aye ga, ke jab azad ham hongey...' The proceedings of the tribunal had to be suspended. When the hearing was resumed the same drama was repeated. Bhagat Singh and his comrades were charged with 'a conspiracy and war against the King Emperor by murder, dacoity and other methods, including the manufacture and use of bombs.' Bhagat Singh was not prepared to defend himself. His father sent a representation to the Viceroy through the tribunal. But Bhagat Singh was unhappy and wrote to his father: 'My life is not precious—at least to me—as you probably think it to be. It is not at all worth buying at the cost of my principles.'

The tribunal found Bhagat Singh guilty in the Lahore Conspiracy Case and sentenced him to be 'hanged by the neck till he is dead' along with Sukh Dev Singh and Raj Guru. Bhagat Singh sacrificed his family attachments for his ideals. For him, the love of humanity subordinated the love for one's family. Independence for mankind was an article of faith with him. For this ideal he willingly and fearlessly walked to the gallows. In the last days of his life, his mind sought contentment in only one thing—the words of a song by Ram Prashad Bismal, which he kept humming all the time: '*Mera rang dey basanti chola, Issi rang mein rang ke Shiv ne maan ka bandhan khola....*'

Bhagat Singh did not appeal for mercy. On the contrary, he appealed for being executed by shooting. He asked the jail authorities that he and his comrades should be treated as political prisoners and not as criminals. He refused to be handcuffed and dressed in black apparel. Addressing the Deputy Commissioner of Lahore, Bhagat Singh remarked: 'Well, Mr Magistrate, you are fortunate to be able today to see how Indian revolutionaries can embrace death with pleasure for the sake of their supreme ideal.' After saying this, Bhagat Singh, Sukh Dev and Raj Guru moved forward to the hangman's platform. In the darkness of the night, the bodies were taken to Gandasingwala in the Ferozepur district. They were together cremated on the shore of the Sutlej and their remains thrown into the river.

Bhagat Singh was fond of reading books. In the condemned cell, he read books on socialism, revolution, communism and history. He is also believed to have written several prose pieces: *Militarism, Why Men Fight, Left-wing Communism, Mutual Aid, Field, Factory and Worship, Civil War in France,*

Land Revolution in Russia, Theory of Historical Materialism, and, *Door to Death, Autobiography, The Revolutionary Movement of India* with biographic sketches of the revolutionaries. Some people say that he sent the manuscripts out of jail through his younger brother who handed them over to a lady for publication. But, somehow, they have never been published.

The ecstatic feelings that Bhagat Singh experienced in kindling the flame of freedom in India and his martyrdom are epitomised in his following words:

Sarfarozi ki tamanna ab hamare dil mein hae
Dekhna hai zor kitna bauzzu-e-qaatal mein hae

[The desire to lay down our lives has grown in our hearts. Now, we have to test how much strength resides in the arm of the killer.]

Bibliography

Adiraju, V.R. *Netaji Subhas Bose*. New Delhi: Om Sree Satya Pub.

Athalye, D.V. *Life of Lokmanya Tilak*. Pune: Annasahib Chiploonkar.

Bhattacharya, Bhabani. *Mahatma Gandhi*. New Delhi: Arnold Heinemann.

Bose, Sisir Kumar. *Netaji Subhas Chandra Bose*. New Delhi: National Book Trust.

Chaitanya, Krishna. *How India Won Her Freedom*. New Delhi: National Book Trust.

Chander, Harish and Padmini. *Dr Shyama Prasad Mookerjee: Contemporary Study*. Delhi: Noida News.

Chari, Seshadri. *Great Life: Shyama Prasad Mookerjee*. Delhi: Gyan.

Das, Sitanshu. *Subhas: A Political Biography*. New Delhi: Rupa.

Deal, G.S. *Shaheed Bhagat Singh: A Biography*. Patiala: Punjabi University.

Deogirikor, T.R. *Gopal Krishna Gokhale*. New Delhi: Pub. Div.

Ferozchand. *Lajpat Rai: Life and Work*. New Delhi: Pub. Div.

Gandhi, M.K. *Autobiography or the Story of My Experiments with Truth* Ahmedabad: Navajivan.

Ghaswala. *Lokmanya Tilak*. New Delhi: Rupa.

Ghosh, A.K. *Bhagat Singh and his Comrades*. New Delhi: CPI.

Guha, Vishnudoe Narain. *M.N. Roy and his Philosophical Ideas*. Muzaffarpur: Shankhanad.

Gupta, A.D. *Subhas Chandra Bose*. New Delhi: Rupa.

Gupta, Manmathnath. *Bhagat Singh and his Times*. Delhi: Lipi.

Hayland, John S. *Gopal Krishna Gokhale*. New Delhi: Rupa.

Jog, N.G. *Lokmanya Bal Gangadhar Tilak*. New Delhi: Pub. Div.

Johar, S.S. *Lala Lajpat Rai*. Jullundur: New Academi.

Johari, J.C. *M.N. Roy: The Great Radical Humanist: Political Biography and Socio-Political Ideas*. New Delhi: Sterling.

Karnik, V.B. *M.N. Roy*. New Delhi: National Book Trust.

Keer, Dhnanjay. *Savarkar and his Times*. Mumbai: V. Keer.

Khergamkar. *Vivekananda*. New Delhi: Jaico.

Kripalani, Coonoor. *Mahatma Gandhi*. New Delhi: Rupa.

Madhok, Balraj. *Portrait of a Martyr: Biography of Dr Shyama Prasad Mookerji*. New Delhi: Rupa.

Mookerjee, Girija Kumar. *Subhas Chandra Bose*. New Delhi: Pub. div.

Payne, Robert. *The Life and Death of Mahatma Gandhi*. New Delhi: Rupa.

Ray, S., (ed.), *M.N. Roy: Philosopher–Revolutionary*. Delhi: Ajanta.

Rolland, Roman. *Mahatma Gandhi*. New Delhi: Rupa.

Roy, Manabindra Nath. *M.N. Roy's Memoirs*. New Delhi: Allied.

Sanyal, Jitendranath. *Amar Shaheed Sardar Bhagat Singh*. Mirzapur: Krantikari.

Sharma, B.S. *Political Philosophy of M.N. Roy*. Delhi: National.

Sharma, O.P. *Great Men of India*. New Delhi: Uppal.

Singh, Swaran. *Path of Revolution: A Biography of Shaheed Bhagat Singh*. Delhi: Wellwish.

Thakur, Gopal. *Bhagat Singh: The Man and His Ideas*. New Delhi: PPH.

Wadia, J.B.H. *M.N. Roy: The Man*. Mumbai: Popular.